Confronting the Storm

Confronting the Storm

Regenerating Leadership and Hope in the Age of Uncertainty

David Ross

BUSINESS EXPERT PRESS

Leader in applied, concise business books

Description

Traditional leadership wisdom is buckling and failing.

Leaders are not only grappling with uncertainty and momentous change resulting from the pandemic, but arguably an even greater storm awaits them—the storm of complex social, environmental, and economic challenges. Welcome to a world that is increasingly volatile, uncertain, complex, and ambiguous.

Normal is never coming back, and leaders and organizations are suddenly extremely vulnerable. This has real consequences for reputation, brand, performance, and—indeed—viability.

But, as daunting as it may feel, the resulting opportunities to thrive are substantial.

David provocatively argues that, to successfully deal with the storm, we must accept that the styles of leadership that have been celebrated for countless years have now become an obstacle—frustrating the delivery of authentic sustainability programs and dragging down organizations and their stakeholders.

He explores storm-defying alternatives: the key skills and traits that are now crucial for regenerating lives, livelihoods, and the planet, pointing the way to a more innovative, successful future for leaders and their organizations.

This argument is amplified by some of the most inspiring senior leaders from across the globe who are successfully confronting the storm. These include a former Prime Minister, former Foreign Affairs Minister, one of *Fortune* magazines "50 Greatest Leaders," and many more. How are *you* confronting the storm?

Keywords

business issues; environmental issues; social issues; innovation; leadership; sustainable development goals; organizational strategy; hope; brand; organizational reputation; uncertainty; VUCA; pandemic

Contents

Testimonials

"Confronting the Storm *is a powerful call for change in the way we view the connection between our institutions, the leadership within, society, and the environment. In these times of uncertainty, it is such a breath of fresh air.*"—**Christelle Vigot, Independent Nonexecutive Director, France**

"*David Ross makes a compelling case for leaders across all sectors to turn and confront the storm. In fact, as a coach who spends much of their time with C-suite leaders, I would suggest* Confronting the Storm *is a mission critical read for you, your organization, and the planet. Eye opening in the extreme.*"—**Cliff Kimber, Executive Coach, The Evolution Partnership Ltd, England**

"Confronting the Storm *is a provocative and thoughtful read on the skills and behavioral traits required to effectively lead in a world rife with complex social, environmental, and economic challenges. David interviewed several prominent global leaders and engagingly communicates their insights about creating a future-focused culture and crew consciousness within organizations.*"—**Bob Leonard, Chief Content Officer, This Spaceship Earth, United States**

"*Author David Ross has penned an impressive landmark missive.* Confronting the Storm *does justice to David's incredible level of perception and emotional intelligence. He sees with clarity the current and emerging issues confronting global society and the skill sets required to be an effective leader.*

The interviews with many and varied leaders from across the world are riveting, sharing insights that are hugely instructive to current and emerging leaders. He convincingly articulates the blueprint to greater levels of collaboration, trust, power sharing, and innovation. I commend the book to you."—**Warwick Giblin, Adjunct Professor and Managing Director, OzEnvironmental Pty Ltd, Australia**

"Confronting the Storm *is a leadership mindset opener in a time when the whole concept of leadership is shifting from mechanistic, hierarchical, and control-based structures to inclusive, dynamic, shared, co-creating experiences.*

A compelling journey on the evolution of leadership, the new critical role of emotional intelligence in the age of uncertainty, and the urgent need of new, even shared and mindful approaches to leading positions in order to serve for a greater purpose.

Timely and Relevant."—**Susana Gago, Founder, Unakti, Spain**

"*Business and society today demand an intellectual ability to span disciplines; the confident dexterity to work within complexity and chaos, while knowing one from the other; and the emotional intelligence to navigate and explore all of the above with those who are right at the coalface of accelerating change. David Ross blends these attributes naturally, with charm and good humor. Driven by deep empathy and intellectual rigor, David's superpower has been his willingness to put in, over decades, the hard work of endless negotiation and learning that underpin this book. His genius—and the genius of this book—lies in sensemaking; through stories, narratives, and experiences that we can identify with and learn from, he both maps where we are and gifts us critical heuristics to guide us forward."*—**Sean O'Sullivan, Founder, Kuné, Ireland**

"*Leadership has never been thought, it has always been about instincts. No wonder most people find it difficult in turbulent times, whether it is environmental crises, COVID issues, or the cause and effects of the Great Resignation. David highlights the real-world problems that leaders are facing and also discusses the solutions. A must read for leaders and aspiring leaders."*—**Vishal Bijlani, Marketing Specialist, India**

Preface

Australia was *burning*. In late 2019/early 2020, my home country felt like it was on fire from one side of the continent to the other. A country that had been unsuccessfully acting on climate change for the past decade was glued to its television screens for many weeks, horrified by what we were watching. We watched the Australian Navy rescue people who were trapped on beaches surrounded by fire, and we watched as the fires were of such an intensity that they created their own weather patterns. Like huge fire tornadoes.

For a people who are used to the traditional summer "fire season," the "Black Summer" fires were of a scale and duration that we had never seen before. If you have never been near a substantial fire, the sky can be an eerie orange to red in color and the smoke so thick that you can't see far in front of you. Indeed, standing at Sydney Harbor, you could see next to nothing of the iconic Harbor Bridge or Opera House nearby.

We are estimated to have lost three billion animals during the fires. Just let that sink in.

Many retreated indoors—call it a lockdown—due to the lingering and thick smoke, concerned about the health impacts.

The population demanded action from our leaders who did little, apart from infuriating many because of their slowness to act, their lack of empathy and competence, and a focus on spinning alternate facts to distract the populace.

I had begun researching this book at the time, while there was a seething fury toward our leaders. There was no way that anything could hold that vehemence back.

And yet ... and yet, at around that time, we were starting to hear about a virus causing difficulties in the Chinese city of Wuhan. Few people, at that time, would have heard of terms like coronavirus, lockdown, and social distancing.

The fury that had been unleashed within Australia and in many parts of the world, demanding action on climate change, dissipated quickly as people switched focus to demanding action from leaders on how to deal with the pandemic. Few leaders appeared able to "walk and chew gum at the same time." As I write, leaders at all levels struggle to genuinely deal with these global problems—and more—with so many in government, business, and in not-for-profits straining, stressing, and just plain hoping that "normal" is right around the corner.

I Haven't Lost Sight of You

Over the coming chapters, I am going to share with you just why "normal" isn't coming back soon. Why it isn't coming back at all.

This has implications for passionate leaders like yourself, now. The story or narrative that you have heard about leadership is out of date. The ways of thinking, doing, and being that have served leaders well for generations have left you exposed to a storm of deeply complex or "wicked" social, economic, and environmental problems. And our world has entered an age of uncertainty, an age that is, and will continue to be, increasingly volatile, uncertain, complex, and ambiguous. This storm already has many leaders lying awake at night. Contrary to what many believe, organizations are not removed or protected from what "lies outside the organization." Not only have society's expectations of institutions—government, corporations, not-for-profits, and even the media—grown as stakeholders become more sophisticated, educated, and coordinated, but the storm creates more significant and interconnected risks that institutions are now susceptible to. I hear those stories, firsthand.

But it doesn't have to be this way. This is a "sliding doors" moment available for leaders to confront and transcend the old ways. What got them to *here*, won't get them to *there*. It is in leaders' interests to gain access to new, resulting opportunities for themselves and their organizations, enhancing innovation, trust, and viability, while also helping to address the worldwide *need* to deal with the storm.

While I am mindful that all leaders have their own skills, experiences, and journeys, I am also going to argue across Chapters 4 to 8 that, in confronting the storm, leaders need to question their personal leadership narrative and worldviews and embark on a more collaborative form of leadership. As we have seen during the pandemic, no leader has all the answers.

I'm also mindful that people hold firm views on how a leader is meant to act or behave. However, few people have the opportunity to see and hear what I experience. And it can be quite shocking. Gone are the days of being able to confront the storm purely with incrementalism or through deploying superficial efforts. Borne out of a passion to serve leaders like yourself, I will even stick my chin out (for a metaphorical hit!) and share my thoughts on what I am seeing and hearing regarding the key skills and behaviors that are necessary for leaders to be successful.

This book is informed by my almost 30 years' working closely with leaders, and organizations and communities of all shapes, sizes, and sectors. Over those years, I have had the privilege of observing, learning, and understanding the context from time spent with amazing people. These people have included C-suite executives in the private sector and senior executives in the public sector through to those without a voice—the poorest members of isolated communities—on the most complex and polarizing of situations and issues.

This book is based on those experiences, listening to bewilderment and confusion from leaders, and frustration (even seething rage) from stakeholders. You won't just read my opinions and what my research shows; threaded throughout are true stories … inspiring insights from some remarkable leaders across the globe on their experiences and simple but powerful ways they confront the storm. You will hear from:

- Former Sierra Leonean Government Minister, Zainab Hawa Bangura
- Latin American Leadership Academy founders, Diego Ontaneda and David Baptista
- EcoPeace Middle East Directors, Gidon Bromberg, Yana Abu Taleb, and Nada Majdalani
- Former Norwegian Prime Minister, Dr. Gro Harlem Brundtland
- One of *Fortune* magazine's "50 Greatest Leaders," U.S. entrepreneur Daniel Epstein from the Unreasonable Group
- The CEO of Swedish company Houdini Sportswear, Eva Karlsson
- Secretary General of the China Biodiversity Conservation and Green Development Foundation, Dr. Jinfeng Zhou

- Chair of the Inuit Circumpolar Council, Dr. Dalee Sambo Dorough
- Faithkeeper of the Onondaga Nation, Oren Lyons

It has been a real privilege to listen to, and learn from, each one of them. To have them convey in some cases just how scary the storm currently is, but to also convey their hope and ways forward.

Finally, I observed that each leader has their own journey and there may be more than one suite of skills and behaviors available to confront the storm. With that in mind, I am offering the opportunity for reflection rather than methodical direction. I humbly offer the following thoughts to trigger reflection within you and/or your organization about why we have an imperative to rethink how we see ourselves and our institutions in relation to our surrounds as well as the regeneration of leadership.

Just what will your legacy be?

David
Sydney, Australia

Acknowledgments

When I set out to write the book, I was so passionate about wanting to make my argument as compelling and engaging as possible. However, it was far more challenging than I had naively imagined. I only got to where I needed to due to the efforts of so many who gave their time and support and who had a belief in what I was wanting to do.

I want to thank Aleks, Andrew, and Isabella so much, without whom this book could, in some ways, possibly feel meaningless to me. Your support and patience are always appreciated.

Anthony "Tone" Bullen has always been there to bounce so many ideas off. I also cannot forget the amazing artwork that he created for the book. Thanks mate!

Through time, I have mentioned to colleagues, friends, and family how each interview felt like it increasingly gave the book "soul." To that end, I sincerely wish to thank Zainab Bangura, Diego Ontaneda, David Baptiste, Gidon Bromberg, Yana Abu Taleb, Nada Majdalani, Dr. Gro Brundtland, Daniel Epstein, Milena Stojceska, Dr. Jinfeng Zhou, Eva Karlsson, Dr. Dalee Sambo Dorough, and Oren Lyons for helping to make the book as engaging as possible with their insights and powerful stories.

A massive thanks must be extended to the ever-patient publishing team at Business Expert Press. That the book has got to this point is reflective of your "superpowers" and support.

There are countless others who I haven't forgotten. David Nussbaum, Tony McGrath, Trish Wilson, John Haughey, and Jason Ardler were helpful with research or with gaining access to interviewees. Bob Leonard and John Groarke looked at earlier versions of the book. Your "eagle eyes" have helped enormously. So, too, there are numerous others who have been there providing interest, counsel, and support as I embarked on this long journey—particularly, Sean O'Sullivan, J. Brian Hennessy, Ian Harris, Mark Downham, Christelle Vigot, Cliff Kimber, Susana Gago, Vishal Bijlani, Warwick Giblin, John Sproule, and Matt O'Neill. Thank you all.

– CHAPTER 1 –

ALREADY,
THE STORM BREWS

We sail within a vast sphere, ever drifting in uncertainty, driven from end to end. When we think to attach ourselves to any point and fasten to it, it wavers and leaves us.

Blaise Pascal

Already, the Storm Brews

As a leader, what is it that you hope to accomplish? Do you find it's getting harder to achieve your dreams? I'm involved in a lot of conversations related to such reflections. So, I want to start by considering the change that has been happening; change that can shape your hopes, one way or another. Regardless of whether the pandemic occurred or not, I will contend across the next three chapters that a momentous storm of social, environmental, and economic issues, existing in an age of uncertainty, was happening anyway. Let's get started.

Just mull over, or reflect on, that last point for a minute. Seismic and turbulent change is already here. Time and again, I see leaders, organizations, and communities that do not recognize that *the storm is here and that we cannot continue to live in the past, calling on old ways of thinking, doing, and being.* I see the difficulties, the stress, and the doubts faced.

From time to time, I am really privileged to be able to work where the policies, strategies, and operations of government and big business intersect with communities, their economies, and the natural environment. This requires me to engage with anyone within a region (some the size of European nations), irrespective of their racial, cultural, or socioeconomic background. I get to listen to executives from the C-suite and the public sector through to those on the margins who are often denied a voice talk about their hopes and their fears for the future. These conversations are, although they don't realize it, about the storm.

When I break this down further, those conversations about the future of society often cover issues concerning their lives, livelihoods, and the planet. We can cover a *vast* range of topics including but not limited to: climate change; conflicts around the lack of access to freshwater; urbanization; economic restructuring; loss of jobs due to automation (and urbanization); concerns for their children's future; polluting the land or water; crime; the plight of Indigenous people; the role of government and business; services for people of all ages; or access to transport, health, and education. And can include the prevailing interconnectedness between *all* of these.

While I will refer to "lives, livelihoods, and the planet," henceforth, I'm referring to a long list of issues pertaining to how people can live happy and stimulating lives, have access to diverse and resilient economies which can provide a good livelihood, and live on a healthy planet that has clean air, water, and soils with a flourishing diversity of plants and animals.

Glorious Pasts

I hear so many stories that never leave me: stories like John's. When I spoke to John, he was in his 70s, living in a remote rural community in Central Queensland, in the north of Australia. I had been engaged by government to advise on developing a long-term strategic plan, 10 years in focus. Part of the project required me to engage with regional communities in many ways including holding group meetings and one-on-one discussions.

I can still picture John walking through the door of a cherished community hall. He was wearing a faded blue work shirt, dirty faded jeans, and an Akubra hat (what many would call a cowboy's hat) that looked enormous. His skin was damaged from working under the harsh Australian sun all his life and he had a no-nonsense attitude. "I'm a straight talker and I'll tell you how it is," he asserted as he shook my hand, making my bones crunch. He was shorter than me but certainly stronger from constant and arduous labor.

As John assumed that I was a government employee (I wasn't), he proceeded to berate me about the government's unwillingness to help the remaining beef cattle farmers, like himself, that made up his small community. The region hadn't had rain for five years. Have you ever been to a community like this? The soil is bone dry; the dust can be so thick on windy days that visibility is reduced to meters. There is a grim resilience on people's faces. What must this do to people's mental health?

John was berating me because he believed that layers of government were doing *nothing* to support the community with respect to the provision of freshwater. He had seen no adaptation in their thinking or actions. People like John had been almost begging for a pipeline to be constructed between a dam approximately 30 km (close to 20 miles) away and his community. The community felt helpless because of the lack of rain and the lack of support or even acknowledgment of their plight from government. And water is life, right?

He was so angry, so frustrated, that he needed to talk *and* talk. I listened for two hours and allowed John to take the conversation wherever he felt it needed to flow. After that, he looked relieved, but spent. (I later found out that I was the first person "from government" to listen to him and he observed that he had told me things that he hadn't told anyone else.)

He didn't feel he needed to say anymore. Yet I had other ideas; I had just one question for him, "Can you tell me what services have been put in place to support people around here with respect to their mental health?" It felt like it took an eternity for John to respond. He looked noticeably deflated and the expression on his face changed. John wasn't looking at me anymore. He was seeing something else, something from the past.

As I write this, I am feeling emotional. For John then told me a story of a work colleague, someone who used to work closely with him and someone who I am sure John cared about. Yet, the people in these communities are meant to be tough and not wanting to show emotions. Emotions are considered to be a sign of weakness. And that's the problem.

John's workmate was subconsciously struggling with the fact that far-reaching change was already here, and that change appeared to be a tiring constant. He was struggling with a lengthy drought and the droughts were occurring ever more frequently. As I see with many people in rural communities, he was also struggling with how urbanization and restructuring of the economy locally, nationally, and globally had affected rural communities like his own. Agriculture continues to play a vital role in developing nations where anywhere between 40 and 90 percent plus of adults in many African nations, for example, and somewhere around 40 percent of adults in southern Asian nations are employed in agriculture. However, it is a different story in developed nations, such as the United States, United Kingdom, and Australia. As countries develop, employment within agriculture drops. This has been the case since the 1950s as the ever-increasing usage of automation on farms in developed nations has reduced employment levels within agriculture to below 10 percent (Roser 2013).

John's mate was struggling. Life and work just felt so grim. Yet, their rural culture required the two men to be "tough." So, they were unable to broach the subject. John thought that something might be on his mate's mind but couldn't bring himself to ask if he was okay; the "elephant in the room" was never acknowledged. One day, his mate took one of his guns, headed for an isolated part of the farm, and having lost all hope, took his own life. He left so many people shocked, saddened, and at a loss. He could no longer locate the region's glorious past that he yearned for.

That John had shared such a personal story with me still feels humbling and a real privilege.

I am frequently told stories like this, and they *never* leave me. These stories aren't just confined to rural communities or even Australia, for that matter.

John then proceeded to tell me how, because of his friend's passing, he has taken it upon himself to make a difference. Grappling with guilt and bewildered by a lack of support from authority, he was using every opportunity at community events to publicly raise awareness about looking after mental health. John is courageous, encouraging people to talk about their problems, and getting communities to realize that admitting you aren't okay does not make you weak. This meant confronting the worldview, the dominant mindset, of the community.

In my many conversations with people from all walks of life about their hopes and fears, conversations often include a yearning for that glorious past—a desire to "return to normal," looking for perspectives, making decisions, or implementing actions that no longer make sense.

But the glorious past isn't returning. It isn't returning for those communities or for the many leaders that I talk to from across public, private, and not-for-profit organizations. Leaders whose thinking and style of leadership is influenced by the weight of history and perhaps the ripples of a glorious past.

Momentous and turbulent change is already here and has implications, positive and negative, beyond anything leaders have dealt with previously. And it *will* continue.

The Age of Uncertainty

The understandable yearning for the past that John's friend and many others desire is exacerbated by the kind of change experienced, as well as the scale of that change. The first time that somebody had formally recognized the hugely significant change we are now experiencing was when academics Warren Bennis and Burt Nanus (1985) referred to it in the mid-1980s. They highlighted how the problems faced by organizations had become increasingly complex and were typified by too many polarities, contradictions, and paradoxes. While these issues were profoundly affecting organizations, Bennis and Nanus noted that institutions were "rigid, slothful, or mercurial" in response.

Organizations hadn't adapted. And maybe they hadn't accepted change was occurring … for many, it can feel like change "creeps up on you." I'm going to illuminate that momentous and turbulent change being observed and the large ripples it creates by introducing you to a few acronyms and an associated term you may not have heard of, namely VUCA; TIMN; and "wicked problems." I suspect that John would have rolled his eyes if I had mentioned these acronyms. You may be feeling that way too. Please humor me and immerse yourself in these acronyms and what they represent because they have implications not only for the Johns of the world and their communities but also for you and your organization too.

VUCA

Bennis and Nanus' observations inspired the U.S. Army War College in the early 1990s to develop a framework to describe a world characterized as being volatile, uncertain, complex, and ambiguous (VUCA) (Yarger 2006). The world wasn't black and white anymore. More was happening. It also became apparent that VUCA wasn't just a concern for military organizations. There were—and still are—significant implications for society, public, private, and not-for-profit organizations.

When people consider volatility, they may think conflict. And there can be a lot of that in an increasingly VUCA world, which I'll delve into in Chapter 3. In this context, however, while conflict is a notable by-product, volatility is intended to convey the explosive speed of change that we are experiencing. Futurist Ray Kurzweil, for example, believes that technological advancement will grow exponentially (Kurzweil 2006). We won't experience one hundred years of technological progress in the 21st century; we will witness the equivalent of 20,000 years of progress, when measured at today's rate (the rate present when he wrote his book). Suffice it to say, he believed that we will experience a rate of technological advancement 1,000 times greater than was experienced in the 20th century. This volatility will understandably leave many stressed or fearful and many in awe of the ceaseless need to adapt or just exhausted, as was the case during the pandemic.

Increased uncertainty implies that there will often be times where we won't be confident in our predictions of how a situation will unfold, even with our intervention. I've listened to a diverse array of leaders who talk about increased uncertainty. They feel like issues they have resolved in the past may reappear but cannot be resolved as confidently as was once the case. "It used to be so much easier, even five years ago. We knew how to fix the issue."

Part of the reason for uncertainly lies in the deep complexity associated with so much that leaders and societies need to deal with. There's a level of intricacy and a sum of too many parts associated with resolving key issues (Yarger 2006). There are many issues where leaders can still resolve a problem, comfortably, based on experience, and there are times when leaders can easily find a way forward to resolving a problem based on their expertise. This is second nature to so many successful leaders. However, leaders are now also required to "dig beneath the surface," to unearth an array of root causes of an opportunity or challenge—all of which need to be tackled. This complexity, often reflective of interconnected issues, reinforces the uncertainty people feel.

Compounding the stress and uncertainty being felt, the speed of change, as well as the belief that things don't seem so simple now, is the ambiguity associated with understanding context. When looking at opportunities and challenges, different people nowadays interpret data in different ways and assign meaning where others see none (Yarger 2006). In Chapter 3, I will delve into the conflicts influenced by the polarized views and interpretations that are present. For leaders, it has become difficult to find a way forward when they don't have confidence in iden-tifying what the problem is, why it is a problem—or whether it actually is *the* true problem. Resolving these problems isn't as likely as it once was. Can you relate to that?

So that's VUCA. It plays a key part in setting the context for our conversation and indeed the context within which leaders make sense of the cues they are receiving, make decisions, and engage with stakeholders about those decisions. Quite rightly, people can suggest that the world has *always* been VUCA. I'm sure that there have always been situations that were volatile or uncertain or complex or ambiguous or a combi-nation of these. The framework, however, suggests that the world has become *increasingly* VUCA; a large part of this has to do with exponen-tial technological advancements as well as the interconnectivity between say, an ever-growing population, societal well-being, and environmental degradation.

As an aside, to give you a sense of just how increasingly volatile, uncertain, complex, and ambiguous the world has become, futurist Jamais Cascio (2020) says that even the term VUCA is no longer adequate to truly describe the extent of what we are facing. Cascio coined a new acronym to describe a world that is now brittle, anxious, nonlinear, and incomprehensible or BANI. What meaning does that have for you?

I don't want you spending too much time absorbing, reflecting on, and assessing the two acronyms. This is not the point I want to share with you. I've introduced VUCA and BANI to get you reflecting on how leaders need to rethink how they make sense of the world in this age of uncertainty and to consider whether the systems of government and busi-ness employing linear thinking and problem-solving mentalities is still relevant. For the sake of brevity throughout the book, I will simply refer to VUCA, rather than BANI (or other similar terms including "TUNA" and "RUPT" to make sense of the change that we are experiencing), as VUCA, at least for now, is more widely known and understood.

Continued Evolution

This brings us to one final acronym which, at a higher level, will play an important part in setting the scene for this book: David Ronfeldt's

(1996) tribes, institutions, markets, and networks (TIMN) framework. I'm introducing TIMN because it goes some way toward understanding the context as to why the world is increasingly VUCA. I'm also introducing it because it plays a part in explaining the tension now faced by leaders who, unsuccessfully, yearn for a glorious past where institutions and market-based private sector companies were seen as the experts in most areas and their judgments weren't questioned.

Ronfeldt's brilliantly developed framework describes how he believes societal evolution has taken place through the ages, and it consists of four basic forms.

- Tribes which are kinship based, expressing an inherent extended family structure. An example would be the fans of a sporting team
- Institutions that are hierarchical in nature, such as government and religious bodies
- Markets which are competitive and respond to the forces of supply and demand
- Networks which are collaborative in nature and are being used successfully by activists and younger generations to progress their goals

The forms are distinctive with respect to the beliefs and values each has and how a system is to be organized; each is easily recognizable along a continuum (Morgan 2020). While versions of each have existed for thousands of years, Ronfeldt believes that each has gained prominence—and dominance—at different rates through time. Tribes (T) developed first before institutional systems (I) allowing T + I societies to form. Societies then enabled the markets to form (M), allowing for tribes (T) + institutions (I) + markets (M) societies to exist before the networks (N) recently began to appear, permitting us to start shifting into T + I + M + N societies. Each form is apparent in different facets of the relevant society.

Each of these forms becomes associated with new capabilities that the predecessor(s) don't possess. As each develops, it enables people to organize to do more than they could previously, notably reducing inefficiencies that had become apparent under the previous dominating form.

As each develops, predecessors cannot thrive the way the newer forms can (Ronfeldt 2016). Their glories are now confined to the past.

The leaders within older forms will also be challenged due to the nature of the key problems faced in a networked, VUCA world. They will be slow to accept or act on the complexities and inefficiencies created by T + I + M societies that the "+N"—the networked societies—will attempt to address. Self-organizing networked groups are already creating new meaning-based governance systems in a response that will be unlike anything prior societies (such as those dominated by institutions and markets) have been able to form (Morgan 2020).

They Ain't Called Wicked for Nothing

I mentioned the number of leaders I talk to from all walks of life who make reference, with a sigh, to how complicated, uncertain, and hostile things can be now. Well, this brings me to the concept of wicked problems. These include but are not limited to local, national, and international issues such as:

- Evolving and migrating demographics
- Rapid urbanization and megacities
- Climate change and resource scarcity
- Shifting centers of power regarding economics and politics
- Rise of technology and connectedness
- Empowered individuals, peak trust, and the era of divisiveness
- Improving—and declining—health and wealth. Inequalities continue to grow in many developed countries as poverty rates remain of significant concern, exacerbating education, health, and well-being opportunities for the disadvantaged (OECD 2016).

Wicked problems aren't solely found on an international scale. Within your local context, there can be discussions about wicked problems such as crime, education, or health. However, and importantly, these challenges—and opportunities—are deeply interconnected. Like VUCA and TIMN, wicked problems have implications for how leaders, well, lead.

They aren't linear in nature like a major construction project or an internal IT upgrade where you can prepare an intricate Gantt Chart and follow that quite successfully to completion. Unlike wicked problems, linear problems are understandable and easy to gain consensus from stakeholders with regard to the causes of the problem and the solution.

Wicked problems don't follow a linear resolution—you cannot solve them, only tame them. Johansen (2007) goes further, observing that these types of problems are more like dilemmas, requiring leaders to *deal* with them rather than solve them. This can mean at times that the preferable decision is the "least worst" option. By the way, Rittel and Webber (1973) classified such problems as wicked because it was apparent that our existing systems were creating problems that these very systems could not solve (Morgan 2020). The systems struggled to acknowledge the existence of these wicked problems. Have things changed?

Rittel and Webber (1973) as well as Camillus (2008) noted that there is an array of reasons why a wicked problem differs from run-of-the-mill problems. These include the notion that:

- It is difficult to define a wicked problem. It never ceases to fascinate me when I ask a diverse group "just what is the problem?" how disparate the responses can be.
- Wicked problems can have several root causes, each of which has a particular value, depending on who you talk to and their perspectives.
- Every wicked problem can, itself, be a root cause of another wicked problem.
- There are no clear and confident solutions to wicked problems. Just as stakeholders can disagree on the problem or its root causes, so too there can be disparities with respect to the way forward.
- Each wicked problem is unique and has no precedent and no clear endpoint. There is little confidence associated with finding a way forward for many.

Our inherent ways of confronting problems just won't suffice when it comes to wicked problems. Instead, things could become worse.

Rather than solving a key or strategic problem on the spot or during a brief brainstorming session, wicked problems highlight that the command and control or heroic style of leadership just won't suffice in these circumstances. More is required with these kinds of challenges than "relying on your gut." This underscores the importance of collaborating, sense-making, and truly trying to understand what is faced by leaders.

The Eye of the Storm

I appreciate that there are some sizeable concepts in this chapter to digest. Does it feel to you like we are experiencing momentous, even turbulent change? I accept that as we all have different perspectives, we may come to different conclusions. Consequently, I have finished off this chapter and forthcoming chapters with a series of question to help you reflect on what these changes I've described mean for your organization, your leadership, and … you.

But, before then, I wanted to share my thoughts on what this all means for lives, livelihoods, and the planet.

Change on any scale can result in leaders running the risk of losing their focus on what is important, strategically, particularly when change occurs at an accelerating rate. Have you heard of the "fire fighters" metaphor? It is used to describe cultures, driven by leaders, that just shift their attention from one issue that is urgent—but often strategically unimportant—to the next urgent but unimportant issue, always focused on quickly solving the issue. Leaders do this at the expense of tackling those issues that are strategically important but not urgent.

We run the risk of taking that approach on a grander scale, resulting in cumulative adverse impacts, particularly when it comes to the wicked— and interconnected—social, environmental, and economic problems that we face. In fact, such cumulative impacts are already present; while many leaders focus solely on the pandemic, climate change (and the other wicked problems mentioned) haven't gone away … in fact, they've grown worse. As change speeds up and becomes more complex, we lose sight of what is important to many people, namely, "home." We lose sight of how to maintain and improve home. Home conjures up several images; to you, it may evoke images of your family, or your literal home, or the surrounding community, and even the natural environment you live in. To John, home meant community as well as his livelihood gained from working the land.

I appreciate that some Eastern nations may be culturally adapted to parts or the sum of the change apparent within VUCA. Charles-Edouard Bouée (2013) notes that Chinese organizations, for example, thrive in a VUCA world due to a dynamism and agility that is culturally considered normal. You will get to read more about this in Chapter 7 when I introduce the courageous Dr Jinfeng Zhou. Nevertheless, globally, we have challenges and opportunities around home, around our lives, livelihoods, and the planet. So, what does this all mean? What do these challenges and opportunities look like? Well, I've really struggled with how to successfully convey this to you. I could share with you countless statistics from international reports or from your own national government's reports, highlighting the scale of the challenges faced. But it is difficult to convey what we face if you have little experience of it. So, instead, here is a unique perspective on these. First, I've listed in Table 1.1 the 17 United Nations (UN) Sustainable Development Goals (SDGs). I hope that you get a sense of the *breadth* of social, economic, and environmental issues facing us. What stands out for you?

Second, I want to introduce you to the groundbreaking and comprehensive planetary boundaries (PB) framework (Figure 1.1). While I had shared the UN's SDGs with you to give you a sense of the breadth

Table 1.1 The breadth of the social, economic, and environmental issues we face

1. No poverty	7. Affordable and clean energy	13. Climate action
2. Zero hunger	8. Decent work and economic growth	14. Life below water
3. Good health and well-being	9. Industry, innovation, and infrastructure	15. Life on land
4. Quality education	10. Reduced inequalities	16. Peace, justice, and strong institutions
5. Gender equality	11. Sustainable cities and communities	17. Partnerships for the goals
6. Clean water and sanitation	12. Responsible consumption and production	

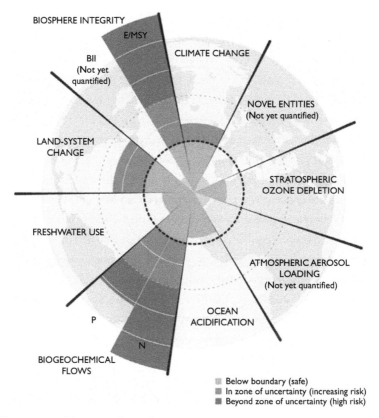

Figure 1.1 Planetary boundaries

Source: Courtesy of J. Lokrantz/Azote based on Steffen et al. (2015).

of issues that we face, and you will shortly hear from an array of leaders to give you depth to the issues faced, hopefully the PB framework will give you a sense of the urgency required. It is a comprehensive early warning system.

To put it simply, the PB framework defines the constraints that we now face at a planetary level to help guide us away from our present, unsustainable, trajectory; that is, it shows where changes are required with respect to critical Earth-system processes if humanity is to continue developing and thriving (Steffen, Richardson, Rockström, Cornell, Fetzer, Bennett, Biggs, Carpenter, de Vries, de Wit, Folke, Gerten, Heinke, Mace, Persson, Ramanathan, Reyers, and Sörlin 2015).

When we look at just one component within the framework, climate change, it is apparent just how urgent is the need for committed and cooperative action. The Intergovernmental Panel on Climate Change (IPCC) has been unequivocal in highlighting what we currently face:

"Human-induced climate change, including more frequent and intense extreme events, has caused widespread adverse impacts and related losses and damages to nature and people, beyond natural climate variability" (IPCC 2022).

Climate change has already disrupted many systems, human, and natural. The impacts are wide-ranging, to say the least. You will hear more about that from several leaders that you will meet throughout the book. Of immediate concern was the recent observation by the IPCC that the evidence of impacts, projected risks, and resulting trends demonstrate that the necessary action required, worldwide, to keep global warming below a 1.5°C increase is more urgent than even they had previously assessed.

While we are clear about the increased risk of climate change to our ability to develop and thrive, the PB framework also highlights that irrespective of the pandemic, systemic risk had been on the rise, often overshadowed by progress in economic development or poverty reductions (UNDP 2020). The increasing risks to humanity are associated with:

- Biosphere integrity, as measured by the rate of extinction of plants and animals as well as the functional diversity of ecosystems
- Biochemical flows exceeding the PB. This refers to: (i) the mining of phosphorus and application of it in the form of fertilizers to erodible soils; (ii) the flow of phosphorus from freshwater systems into the ocean; and (iii) the industrial use of nitrogen in fertilizers
- Land-system change, as measured by the area of forested land as a percentage of the original cover, for example (Steffen et al. 2015).

What concerned me when I read the associated report is that, at present, the experts are unable to quantify the risks associated with "novel entities." This could include chemicals or other new types of engineered materials or organisms, each of which could have the potential to create adverse impacts on vital processes from their persistence and mobility.

Imagine the vast amount of chemicals or materials this could include? Think about the concerns being raised in the last few years about the scale of the distribution of micro-plastics across the world. Current modeling suggests we could ingest 20 kg or over 40 lb. of microplastics during our lifetime. Who knows how this could affect humanity and the planet?

Remember that everything covered in the PB framework does not exist in isolation from one another. These overly complex processes are highly integrated, with interactions that cause unintended consequences. In just over a decade, we experienced "the global financial crisis, the climate crisis, the inequality crisis, and the COVID-19 crisis," not to mention the increasing rate of extinction of wildlife crisis. All of these have "shown that the resilience of the system itself is breaking down" and, potentially, trigger the tipping points from which we cannot recover. Faced with interconnected social imbalances and planetary pressures, this emphasizes the need for systems thinking and the need to avoid a reductive approach as has been the case with linear problem solving (Steffen et al. 2015; UNDP 2020). We need to "rattle the cage" and appreciate that we need to treat the system and leadership differently.

It is also worth highlighting that these calls, challenging how we treat the planet and each other, aren't just coming from civic leaders or scientists. Religious leaders have also called for improvements to "home." Pope Francis, for example, made an urgent appeal for the protection of the home common to all of us. He implored the need to "bring the whole family together to seek a sustainable and integral development, for we know that things can change … Humanity still has the ability to work together in building our common home" (Pope Francis 2015).

It can feel difficult to convey a clear sense of what the storm looks like if your only feedback is from mainstream media. Realizing that I needed assistance in this regard, I've called on some amazing leaders to explain the storm from their perspectives. Subsequently, I am really excited to introduce you firstly to the truly inspiring Zainab Bangura.

What a powerful story she has. Key to the conversation I am having with you is *part* of her background as a women's rights campaigner and activist. Up until 2002, Sierra Leonean women and girls were endangered by widespread and systematic sexual violence, including rape and sexual slavery. Zainab became prominent during this time documenting, monitoring, and reporting such horrendous crimes and other human rights violations (Sambira n.d.). Through time, she progressed to becoming the Sierra Leone Foreign Minister, then Minister for Health and Sanitation before continuing her committed service to Africa, and the wider globe in roles including, but not limited to, the second UN Special Representative on Sexual Violence in Conflict. That role reflects the passion that she has for gender equality and the power of education. Just imagine what she has heard, seen, and felt.

My conversations with Zainab left me speechless and numb at times with respect to what she shared. I challenge you to feel otherwise.

Now, when organizations think about, say, climate change, they may think only about direct impacts resulting from dealing with extreme temperatures or declining or extreme rainfall events. Yet, as Zainab noted, there are momentous indirect impacts that we must confront. "You know, look at the Sahel (the semiarid transitional band south of the Sahara that extends from Sudan and Eritrea in the east to Mauritania and Senegal in the west). The reality is the Sahara Desert is expanding. You have the pastoral people who don't respect international borders; they go where the water is to feed their cattle. So, they encroach into other areas."

"And this is what we're witnessing in a lot of countries. They have no respect. They follow the water, and the water beds are shrinking, drying up ... creating conflict. It's affected social cohesion between people who used to live together and so, it is less predictable. You are having less predictable rainfall, more droughts, and these borders with the desert are shrinking. It's in the Sahel, it's here, between Kenya, South Sudan, Somalia, South Sudan. All of that area. Climate change is causing these conflicts—and to understand that (extremist organization) Al Shabaab is operating in Somalia, and people must come there with their cattle looking for water. It's a big crisis, that is in full swing. That's the reality."

Yet, climate change isn't creating seismic impacts in isolation from other challenges. The Sahel is particularly vulnerable. It is a region subjected to many interconnected, complex challenges. These include civil unrest, high population growth, and food and water insecurity. As IEP (2021) observe, ecological degradation and population growth in the Sahel have *increased* the likelihood of conflict.

Zainab provided a human side to how the COVID-19 pandemic is also exacerbating the quality of African lives and livelihoods. She noted that, to understand the context faced, it is worthwhile appreciating that the 17 SDGs were developed to address the problems that "have always been there. What the pandemic has done is exacerbated the problems for us. If you take health care, we've always known that we have a problem. What the pandemic has done for us is to show how inadequately we have funded the health care system, how we've neglected it. COVID also highlighted some of the things that we did not think at the time were issues. If you take the economy in Africa, what the pandemic is doing is making the economy collapse. In a country like Kenya where I am, over 30% or more of their GDP is hospitality. Now when you shut down the country, no tourists are coming in. If the economies of the West are under a lot of strain, how do you think they're going to invest into Africa? These are the discussions we are not completely awakened to."

"I think that what has come out of the pandemic for Africa, is that it has highlighted our weaknesses, our vulnerability, the inequality, and the injustice of the global system as it relates to Africa. We couldn't meet the SDGs on education, on reduction of poverty, most people have gone under poverty during this time because there's a lot of unemployment. Jobs have been lost, companies have closed, you know, children cannot go to school. That's what has been highlighted. We have to start a new thinking, we have to think internally and say, 'how can we make sure we do not become more vulnerable?' We cannot depend 100% on a global system. We have to develop a system that will allow us, in the most difficult circumstances, to survive."

You may feel removed from what Zainab has seen in Africa. However, I believe that there is much that can be related back to the situation that any institution finds itself in. Just like Africa, organizations are finding themselves exposed to more conflict, and many institutions have been found to be brittle in response to the pandemic and climate change. They have been exposed, needing new ways of thinking, new leadership styles. Even business models that were appropriate 10 years ago may no longer be appropriate in an age of uncertainty.

Yet, even with the seismic hardships Zainab identified that are facing Africa—*even then*—you aren't getting a sense of the extensive interconnectivity that can adversely impact upon lives, livelihoods, and the planet in *so many* ways. Just as when you descend in a plane through the clouds and you suddenly see the extensive detail of a city or town below, so too once you drill down further, you really get a sense of what is apparent.

I wanted to learn more about how *just* these two issues alone—the pandemic and climate change—are affecting so many of Africa's women and girls.

Firstly, the short- to long-term impacts on girls are utterly profound and profoundly worrying. "Some girls, some of them have lost years, which they will not regain. There is early pregnancy. Or, in the villages they force their children to get married, instead of getting pregnant." So, they won't return to getting an education and will be lost to the workforce or creating their own opportunities for the workforce. Just imagine how society is missing out from not having access to these great minds or potential leaders? I will expand on this in the next chapter from a Latin American perspective. But there is even more to it than that.

"In a lot of the schools, children get their main meal in school. So, when the schools are closed, these children are deprived of the main meal they have. Imagine the consequences on the girl child, in terms of the lockdown, the ability to go to school, the ability to feed them. You have a whole generation that is going to drop out." The consequences are unfathomable. It deeply pains me to say that it is just as difficult for women. "If you take the informal (employment) sector in Africa, it's dominated by women. This is a sector where they don't get access to support systems. So, they have not been working in the informal sector, as it only succeeds on a thriving economy. You have more women in social services, in-house, in education, in the hospitality industry and these are where the pandemic has hit considerably."

"So girls have become pregnant—but don't even talk about domestic violence," Zainab asserted. "In Kenya, the record shows that increased by 40%. The husband has lost their job; he cannot feed his wife. Of course, tempers are high, the men become abusive and hit the women to deal with their own frustration. It has been very difficult during the pandemic. I think for me, as a woman, I was able to respond. I was able to understand because I had been in an abusive relationship."

Anyway, that won't be the last we hear of Zainab's story throughout the book. There's more.

Due to the increasing interconnectedness that we are experiencing from living in a networked world, I am going to argue that organizations, irrespective of the sector that they operate in, are not isolated from the social, economic, and environmental challenges and the associated, far-reaching, and complex change that is occurring. Organizations are not an island unto themselves. Even if consideration is given to just one of the megatrends, climate change, it is apparent that more proactive, anticipatory, and adaptive approaches are required if organizations are to survive and thrive.

Finally, do you remember Kurzweil's expectations that the world will experience 1,000 times the technological advancements this century as experienced in the last? This means that all these implications I've described will get more complex and disruptive. As I've noted, this has profound consequences for organizations. In Chapter 2, I am going to talk about what this really means for leaders, their leadership styles and how this translates to their efforts to deal with external issues, those influencing the quality of lives, livelihoods, and the planet.

Reflections

As you progress through the reflections at the end of each chapter, please grab a pad and pen and *take your time*.

What has change looked like, or felt like, for you over the past two years? Over the past five years? What change if any have you noticed with respect to:

- Your local, national, and global economy? Is the makeup of industries changing? Are the industries or companies that dominated five years ago still dominant?
- Social issues? Have new social issues or movements risen? What is being questioned or confronted regarding once taken-for-granted values and beliefs?
- Technology? Are you seeing at least some of what Kurzweil wrote about?

- Environmental issues? What environmental issues are now a strategic risk for your organization? Does your risk register needs revision?

What implications does this kind of change have for your organization? Or you? Does it feel like change is speeding up? Similar to what Zainab said about Africa, does your organization feel vulnerable?

How has your organization responded to wicked problems?

Have you worked in an organization that was focused on a glorious past? What did that look like? What did leadership in the organization look like?

– CHAPTER 2 –

BLISSFULLY UNAWARE
OF THE DARK CLOUDS

Humankind has not woven the web of life. We are but one thread within it. Whatever we do to the web, we do to ourselves. All things are bound together. All things connect.

Chief Seattle

Blissfully Unaware of the Dark Clouds

Having just shared with you the context within which leaders now find themselves in, this chapter starts with my view on what has got the dominant styles of leadership, broadly, to where they are now. I will also discuss the challenges that historical behaviors create for leaders with respect to genuinely confronting the storm. This is crucial for being able to lead successfully in this age of uncertainty.

Leadership is now being called into question within our media and wider societies. Why do you think this is? Do you feel that sustainability and sustainable development issues are tackled authentically and successfully within our institutions? Do you think that has played a part, directly or indirectly, in leadership being questioned? Let's explore that now.

Anchored to the Past

Even without consideration of the momentous and interwoven change that we are experiencing throughout this age of uncertainty, we run the risk of remaining anchored to behaviors that were appropriate in the past but now seem to have little rhyme or reason. From a leadership perspective, we run the risk of not readily adapting to what we are now experiencing—like the boiling frog syndrome.

This anchoring of behaviors started from the earliest stories within humanity. Certainly, stories have played a huge part within civilizations going back millennia as they are a fundamental part of our humanity. Stories provide us all with inspiration, entertainment, a sense of identity, meaning, and purpose. A fundamental story, for centuries, has been the hero's journey. The hero, be they a hunter, on a military field, or a captain of industry, was always the leader and the leader was always the hero. The stories were important to the collective. The hero, the leader, was in unquestioning control (Kakabadse 2000).

Yet, these stories that carry great power do not always ring true. We make assumptions about the leader being strong, brave, and always knowing what to do. I was fascinated to read that the legendary Sun Tzu's great grandson, Sun Pin, wrote in the 4th century BC that effective leadership requires more than just the deployment of authority that comes with being the hero. What do you make of that? Leaders, observed Sun, need to look after their followers—probably what we would call stakeholders today—and their needs. This required a more interpersonal approach, seeing followers as valuable assets (Rarick 2007). Personally, I find it surprising that such views underpinned by what we would now call facets of emotional intelligence were being raised in the 4th century BC!

It is also worthwhile noting that there are many stories about "the wisdom of our elders" and consequently, embedding the role of the elder as the leader and "the voice of sense." The elders brought peace between warring sides. Peace achieved through influence, mediation, and calmly viewing different perspectives. The elders were admired for bringing back day-to-day normality (Kakabadse 2000). Perhaps, you can think of notable examples of such leaders.

Nowadays, in my wide-ranging interactions, I am fascinated with the continued strength of these stories and how embedded they are. I see many heroic leaders, many command-and-control leaders, and many older leaders. I feel for them as they struggle with the speed of change now faced. I do not doubt the worth of these stories but question their validity in many circumstances. I see how we are missing out on involving different perspectives, much to our detriment. For example, the capabilities and value of younger leaders are often called into question. Having listened to many, I believe that many younger leaders are often most impressive. We are missing out not only on diverse perspectives but also on additional resources and innovations, to say the least. Is this really a problem if we continue adhering to the old stories of leadership? What do you think? Think of it this way: Ronfeldt's TIMN framework suggests that society has fundamentally changed through time to being more networked. The megatrends suggest that significant social, economic, and environmental change is globally occurring, creating an array of formidable issues *and* the increasing VUCA we are experiencing suggests that the change is far-reaching. The rate of change is ever-growing. Yet, leadership does not appear to have broadly kept up with these changes.

There are strategic implications from these holdover leadership styles. Of relevance to the argument that I am making are the following:

- Many well-meaning and caring people are grappling with systemic problems. Of note in the private sector is confusion about why corporations exist. Do they exist to create short-term shareholder value? Or longer-term value to stakeholders? Was it economist Milton Friedman who had stated that "the only business of business is business"? Yet, commentators like Fullerton (2015) have been dismissive of what this has created:

  "The take-make-waste design of work has left in its wake a crescendo of interconnected environmental crises threatening to undermine the very foundation of the economic system itself. We are destroying the planet because there is a profit in it." What do you think should be consigned to the past?

- Previously, I shared with you Ray Kurzweil's views on technology and its mind-boggling rate of acceleration. He also observed that this rate of change is deceiving, starting off "imperceptibly and then explodes with unexpected fury." Leaders are waiting too long to pivot or adapt. And that has something to do with their inability to deal with wicked problems and how slowly worldviews adapt to change.

- The inability to deliver "higher-order desires" due to lapses in judgment or a weakness of will. Whose purpose have many leaders been serving? The collective? Shareholders? Or just their own?

- Regrettably, but not surprisingly, an avoidance of the facts. This is due to siloed thinking or due to groupthink stemming from a *desired* lack of inclusion in decision making (Kurzweil 2006; Allio 2007). The only voices listened to were those who supported the leader.

When I listened to the stirring Diego Ontaneda and David Baptiste speak, I quickly gained from their perspectives an insight into how these holdover leadership stories seem to have failed many younger people across Latin America, for example. For it was, in essence, those stories and how they play out that compelled Diego and David to develop the Latin American Leadership Academy (LALA) in the first place to help younger people reach their potential.

David was impassioned in his observations of what younger people experience. "When I talk about Latin America, it has the greatest social and economic gap in the world, some argue. You have the richest of the rich. You have an infrastructure in some places that rivals the first world and yet, so many are left behind."

Inequality is purported to be one of the most distinctive characteristics of Latin American economies, leading to low productivity and low economic growth. Yet, as will be conveyed by Diego and David, this isn't just about income equality; women face an unlevel playing field in the workforce. Ethnic minorities lack access to basic service (UNDP 2021).

To give a deeper sense of the inequality, David talked about social mobility, highlighting what had been observed in a recent OECD report. Namely, that today's socioeconomic inequalities have huge implications for the affected with respect to not only getting ahead but also access to education, health, and the labor market (OECD 2018). "Social mobility," David continued, "looked at the number of generations from the bottom of the social and economic graph to do with just normal drift … like you wake up the one day and think 'how many generations does it take to get to the middle (of the graph)?' Denmark: two generations. World average: four and a half. US: four and a half, five. It's a long time. Cut to Latin America. Brazil? Nine generations. Colombia: 11 generations! It might as well be never."

That one statement started to convey to me the scale of what is faced, there. This issue of low social mobility has been a problem, worldwide, particularly since the early 1980s. It means that children born into the bottom of the income distribution have less chance to move up and improve their lives and earnings than their parents. They're trapped. From an economics perspective, lack of upward mobility for the younger people in Latin America also means that many talented people miss out on gaining development. Subsequently, there are flow-on effects to many investment opportunities going unexploited and potential businesses never seeing the light of day (OECD 2018). Low social mobility also means reducing the opportunities, innovations, solutions, and resources available to confront the storm.

Yet, if that isn't concerning enough, David highlighted how he believes that even OECD (2018) only tells part of the story. "What's most impactful about that study is what's missing from it. Race is not factored in. And so when you think about the social and economic gaps, and how the cycles are being propagated in the system that we have, who gets the opportunities, where is the investment going, … it's inclusion that is top of our mind, and how to break the vicious cycles of entrapment that we see in the region."

How could issues like this affect organizations and the economy in your part of the world?

Diego and David are actually working to ensure that future generations have the ability to meet their own needs rather than continue to fall through the gaps. "There's an opportunity here to create a first generation of high impact protagonists and find alternative paths to success, where young people are able to embrace a more holistic and healing solution to the generational trauma of the historical injustices of the past," observed Diego. As an aside, I really liked his reference to "healing solutions." I see that trauma at, or near, the surface all the time. I see the resulting conflict, too.

Diego and David are passionate about changing the landscape of the region, developing an abundance of well-developed younger people, because they believe that the current system is allowing too many to fall through the cracks. Subsequently, they set about transforming education for younger people, scaling an education model that is evidence based and specific to Latin America's context (LALA 2021). "I ended up in the camp of people that had access to the best education, the best networks, and so on," observed Diego. "And just being one more on the pile, who used that for his own benefit, for me, took on a tinge of … this is wrong. I heard about African Leadership Academy and their model of finding young leaders all over Africa—the whole systemic, socioeconomic spectrum—and empowering them to solve the problems that they were seeing in their communities. I was like, 'this is something that is breaking away from the previous models'. This is unique, right?"

He and David brought the model to Latin America rather than rely on the legacy leadership stories that I've been discussing. "Instead of choosing one issue to tackle, I could help empower young leaders to solve the problems in their own communities. That struck me as the most authentic, scalable, and sustainable way to change the world" (LALA 2021).

Another fundamental explanation underpinning the holdover leadership styles I referred to above is our dominant mindsets or worldviews, which downplay issues to consolidate our stories. Worldviews like "*we know what is best for younger people*," as was implied to me by Diego and David; these dominant mindsets play a central part in this book going forward.

Moving on, I have no doubt that leaders have always had notable challenges. However, by the 1970s, it had become apparent that organizations were operating within a changing context where it wasn't only tame problems that had to be dealt with. Wicked social, economic, and environmental problems were already occurring, bearing challenges for organizations and their leaders. In such a context, what got leaders to "here" was most certainly not going to get them to "there."

So, did we tackle these with a genuine commitment?

The Efforts of the Cynical

Social and environmental issues gained greater attention within society after Rachel Carson wrote her ground-breaking *Silent Spring* in 1962. While there were other "triggers," her book inspired more than a movement. Starting off in the United States, it facilitated changes within the thinking of society and then governments across the Western World concerning pollution and, to an extent, the depletion of natural resources. This was an important starting point to tackle an array of social and environmental issues.

Through time, awareness within society continued to grow of the changes that were either already being experienced or were forecast. Remember that global warming was on the radar of multinational energy companies since the 1970s. So, too, depletion of the ozone layer created global discussion about the impact humanity was having on each other and the planet. Change was also being observed in global populations and what they valued (Tibbs 2011). Changing values within society is a vital component of the context when I mention the growth of outrage and the decline of trust in our institutions.

In 1983, the UN General Assembly called for a "global agenda for change" to consider how the international community could better deal with social and environmental issues. This was the responsibility of the then-formed World Commission on Environment and Development, chaired by Norwegian Dr. Gro Harlem Brundtland, who went on to be a three-term Prime Minister. The Commission's efforts were submitted to the UN General Assembly as the "Our Common Future" (or the so-called Brundtland) Report. A key point made by the Commission in its report was as follows:

Humanity has the ability to make development sustainable to ensure that it meets the needs of the present without compromising the ability of future generations to meet their own needs
—Brundtland Report 1987

While governments had programs in place related to the protection of lives, livelihoods, and the planet, it could be argued that the Brundtland Report was *the* catalyst for modern-day sustainability, triple bottom line (TBL), corporate social responsibility (CSR), and sustainable development programs within the private and public sectors. Some organizations have continued to run sustainability programs ever since that point. They were exciting times—times when companies were first exploring resource and material efficiency programs and eventually environmental footprint or life cycle analysis programs, aiming to find out which parts of their organization created the most sizeable impacts upon the planet and then do something about it. It was a way to reduce costs and create a point of differentiation. Awareness grew and grew quickly. Government agencies also explored ways that they could support the private sector through funding, advocacy, or training. With this increased "maturity" came further advancements in social justice and human and ecological resilience. Yet, many people, including myself, see how sustainability efforts have now evolved: to become little more than the application of a bandage on a large, extraordinarily deep wound.

I agree with Gibbons' (2020) analysis that the sustainability field has been unsuccessful in positively shifting those social and environmental trajectories. This "(un)sustainability" that Gibbons refers to is a consequence of a predilection on incrementalism and on addressing symptoms rather than root causes to "enable continuous economic development within a context of finite resources." It was about specifically sustaining business as usual.

And for executive members, make no mistake, their efforts were—and still are, on many occasions—seen by stakeholders for what they were: nothing more than greenwash. That is, deeply cynical marketing efforts to portray organizations to be something that they weren't—socially, economically, or environmentally mindful. These behaviors need to be relegated to the past. As these issues grow in scale and complexity, so too, the murmurings and concerns within society progressively grow, unabated. How could these programs remain so superficial in their outputs and outcomes while organizational leaders believe that it wouldn't be seen as such by the wider community?

It's seen by LALA, leaving David extremely frustrated.

"There's not enough localization of initiatives, not enough building of real capacity and leadership and ownership in different communities. There's a lot of imposition of, like, 'Oh, this is what *you* need'. And, you know, at its most dramatic, you end up with the images of abandoned tractors and abandoned wells all over Africa; I've had the extreme version of these going wrong." David was frustrated with how many leaders in Latin America are either unable or unwilling to change the status quo. "At the other end of the spectrum, you have grassroots movements—and they've also mostly been unable to change the systems. They're disconnected from the best talent, the latest knowledge, disconnected from each other. So, there's a lot of duplication of efforts, a lot of fragmentation."

Diego highlighted why younger Latin Americans are so cynical. "It's not just income inequality. Educational inequality is dramatic. On top of that, you have widespread sexism, racism—all sorts of forms of discrimination. Think about what that does to people's belief in the system, in getting out of poverty through hard work, through formal channels that are broken, or closed for most. Think about what that does to generations after generations of broken promises. These teenagers are trying to fight these fights, holding on to hope by a thread, and also knowing that chances are, most of them are going to actually lose that fight. There's a cost to not acting. Now it's untenable."

Because of how this plays out in Latin America and the impacts observed there, David was quite challenging *yet* also, motivating, in his advice to leaders. "The power you wield is enough to make a difference. And you have the powers available. You can't go 'Oh, there's nothing I can do about it'. There are things that you *can* do about it. And we need to be more aware of what those things are because these deficit conditions are growth conditions if we can be smart about setting goals, objectives, and a certain kind of priority."

We need to rethink our efforts. We need to transcend sustainability and reflect more on what we collectively value. Just as I noted that there are some who feel that the term VUCA does not go far enough in helping us gain strategic insights into what we are increasingly experiencing, so too there are those who believe that the term sustainability is now inadequate. I believe that the term has been sullied by the superficial efforts of so many organizations. What has been realized is that these efforts need to be working toward something far more significant. In the current context, it is about working systemically toward strengthening that which underpins the health, quality of life, and resilience of the planet to ensure that life, including our own, doesn't just survive but flourishes (Wahl 2018).

A different way is desperately needed. We'll explore that further in Chapter 4.

Nevertheless, there are real benefits to your organization from undertaking genuine contributions to transform and transcend sustainability to move toward regenerative practices. Such practices move beyond existing concepts of efficiency or "net zero" to consider how human activities can actively redress the damage imposed on human and ecological communities and contribute to ongoing improvement. Regenerative practices shift the thinking from scarcity to abundance (Camrass 2020; Hahn and Tampe 2021). In doing so, is a reliance on 20th-century thinking still appropriate while our context rapidly changes?

I promise that I will talk more about "the why"—why the shift is necessary—in the next chapter and bring it all together in Chapter 4, where I will deliver the findings of my research regarding what transformational leadership will need to draw on to ensure that organizations remain viable in the long term.

Before I cover that, I want to spend time exploring how these unsuccessful efforts, to date, to shift leadership styles and organizational priorities also take place in a context a lot closer to home—in each and every one of us.

Held Back by Ourselves

Certainly, it could be argued that sustainability efforts have always run the risk of being unsuccessful because programs often lack alignment with corporate strategy in the private sector. Causes have often been irrelevant. And in the case of government, one or more of the following: politicians not dealing with difficult and contentious policies for fear of not being re-elected, incoherent, and superficial policy or not accepting that there will never be enough resources to do everything and subsequently, agencies spreading their efforts too thin.

Even though Diego and David see how the old, embedded stories of leadership around sustainability and sustainable development adversely impacted on younger generations across Latin America, they still have real hope. As I had observed, young leaders are so impressive; their combination of a critical eye and a hopeful heart is so vital in instigating positive change (Ganz 2009).

That is a critical message to take away at this point.

"The very thing that has created the vicious cycle," noted David, "creates an opportunity for transformation. It can be the bystander effect where everyone just sits there and does nothing; it's tragic. Or one person can act, and suddenly, everyone's acting, and the forces are bigger than we are. Those conditions for the vicious cycles—that scarcity—can turn on its head and create wild abundance. It's our job to figure out which interventions they need—what are the pathways and we're getting better at it." And it sounds like, through taking a holistic approach to this younger generation of Latin American leaders rather than a superficial effort, the outcomes with respect to confronting the storm have been absolutely inspiring.

"One story that we love to share," smiled Diego, "is of Julia. She's a student who grew up in a favela in Rio de Janeiro. She started selling chocolates in the street at age 13 to 14. And you ask her, 'Why did you start so young?' She's like 'What? So that my sister didn't have to!' And you're just in tears. Single mom, she was paying rent and electricity by 15. Had bad grades in school because she was not sleeping. She was staying up late and then waking up early to make the chocolates, go out and sell the chocolates, and so on."

Things have changed for the better for Julia due to the support of LALA. Diego continued, "She's now trilingual. After a lot of programs, she wrote to us three months later, and she told us that she just read 25 books. And then she added 'It's not just that I read 25 books. I've *healed* my relationship with books because before, it was traumatic'. She got into Babson College; that's a $300,000 scholarship!"

"She launched a social enterprise, empowering women in Brazilian prisons to produce organic, usable women's cotton menstrual pads and raised something like $7,000 in two weeks. For context, her mom makes probably $200 a month. She's exceptional. But she's not the exception. We now believe there's 100s if not 1,000s of kids just like that."

For all of the positive efforts of the Diegos and Davids of the world, there is too often something much deeper that has a bearing on global sustainability efforts to date. When we consider leadership in relation to sustainability, sustainable development, and CSR efforts, it is not only history and its influence that we must consider. We must also consider ourselves and the "constructed environment" within which we work.

Our Worldviews

We grapple with so much information, even before we had to deal with recent, explosive advancements in technology. This makes it difficult to absorb, reflect on, and make sense of all that we experience. It is just not possible for the brain to grasp all of what we receive.

Instead, we have lenses through which we view our world. They help us make sense of the world, creating meaning and purpose for us. Borne out of our individual experiences, that is our worldview. They color the way that we see the world. With respect to all that we are taking in, they prioritize particular cues over others that we receive, determining our priorities and reinforcing our "view of reality and of what is true and right" (Valk, Belding, Crumpton, Harter, and Ream 2011). And we all behave, function, and importantly, *lead* according to the worldviews that we hold. Since these worldviews or mindsets are borne out of our individual experiences, we all come to any situation with different worldviews. Yet, there are often dominant worldviews within cultures that influence our own thinking and behaviors.

They influence our style of leadership and decision making. You will recall that I've briefly introduced the TIMN framework. While we are living in an increasingly networked world, we are still heavily influenced by our legacy worldviews and ways of thinking borne out of a reverence for institutions and more recently, markets. That is, we are unconsciously influenced by the hierarchies established by institutions like government, corporations, and religious bodies, as well as a laser-like focus on markets.

Certainly, different civilizations and cultures exhibit different worldviews, with some considered to have more appropriate characteristics for the momentous change we are experiencing (Eidelson and Eidelson 2003). These influences can have profound implications for how society and therefore leaders respond to sustainability and sustainable development issues. In the case of the Western worldview, there are those who have been extremely critical, believing that there is a dysfunction that has resulted in a breakdown of the legitimacy of Western ways (Ramos 2003). I know this is provocative, and you may even be wondering why I bring it up. To try and explain why, I'll share with you common worldviews that I encounter with respect to lives, livelihoods, and the planet. These can come from quite different perspectives and cultures, namely:

- *We* know what's best for you (don't question us).
- The economy is a machine that society needs to continue fueling.
- Alternatively, society is fueled by the economy. Jobs give us meaning, identity, and money to maintain or enhance the quality of our lives.

- The environment is a machine that we have mastery over and can pull apart and put back together again. The land is a resource to be exploited.
- Alternatively, the environment is extraordinarily complex and interwoven and we are dependent on it. The land is sacred. We are immersed in it and are its stewards.
- Wisdom resides with our elders (younger people should just be quiet).
- Similarly, wisdom resides with "us," not "them" (whether this relates to race, class, gender, or generation).

Can you just read through this list one more time for me? Do you see some expressions there that reflect your own worldview or those of "influencers" within your organization? That's natural! When people share their worldviews with me in relation to their hopes and fears, these conversations are instructive at emphasizing how the worldviews of decision makers within government and corporations can, unwittingly, adversely affect the lives of people within society. Substantially, not all those worldviews I have listed are dominant.

In Chapter 3, I will follow up on this topic and discuss the implications for reputations and brands, trust in them, and conflict or outrage. I see a lot of outrage nowadays that is directed at government, government agencies, and corporations—a lot.

Worldviews are also important to consider because, through the provision of meaning, they can help or hinder our ability to see a bigger picture—like how our leadership may affect lives, livelihoods, and the planet. Remember John the cattle farmer from Chapter 1? John framed what he told me as his truth. In his mind, and for so many of us, we think that our worldview is the one that reflects reality. Yet, how can there be so many conflicting versions of reality? Hence, as I observed above, irrespective of what may reflect your worldview, there is no judgment associated with what I am discussing. It just "is." Unless we question the dominant worldviews within our organizations and whether a lack of diverse, inclusive perspectives is an issue, we won't appreciate whether they create positive or adverse impacts.

And, as I am about to show you, if we don't question the dominant thinking in our organizations, leaders run the sizeable risk of having to face costly, damaging, long-term outrage and mistrust. The consequences are overwhelming.

Reflections

What is the dominant story about leadership in your organization? Does it reflect 20th-century thinking? Is that appropriate as we experience momentous change?

What does sustainability or CSR look like in your organization? Is it an awkward, greenwashed add-on solely for short-term profits?

Has *genuine* value been placed within your organization on lives, livelihoods, and the planet? Has sustainability or CSR helped your organization maintain a sterling reputation?

Consider your organization's culture. What are the prevalent worldviews and values? How do these influence decisions around lives, livelihoods, and the planet?

Do you think that level of exasperation is only "localized" to Latin America? What do you see with your own organization? Is conflict "waiting" for you?

How do you think that momentous change could impact dominant worldviews in your organization? Could they change at all?

Ask yourself, "What does my worldview look like? How do I respond to the worldviews of others?"

– CHAPTER 3 –

THUNDER RUMBLES
NEARBY

The difficulty lies not in the new ideas, but in escaping from the old ones.

John Maynard Keynes

– CHAPTER 3 –

Thunder Rumbles Nearby

Having shared with you my views on how traditional leadership and the superficial approach taken by many to sustainability and CSR programs in the context of the age of uncertainty, it is time to highlight the ramifications. It's going to get a little bumpy.

Before I discuss this, just what role have the dominant worldviews in your organization had when it comes to contributing to improving lives, livelihoods, and the planet? And strategically or tactically, has this had implications for the organization? Or for you?

Don't get me wrong. The traditional approaches to leadership were appropriate for *that* time. Perhaps, the challenge for many leaders now is appreciating that our organizations, our institutions, also experience adverse consequences from an inability to confront this storm positively and profoundly. "No man/woman is an island," as it were. Therefore, I will build on what we've talked about to date, describing what the wider society is experiencing with respect to our institutions, how it makes them feel, and the commercial impacts.

Whatever complex issues are playing out, they don't do this in isolation of one another. Instead, because issues are often within an array of interconnecting ecosystems (natural and human), they can reinforce one another, further exacerbating the challenges society faces.

Perhaps, you feel that there is a lot happening or changing locally, nationally, and globally, which is external to your organization and will not affect your bottom line or reputation. As we have seen with the pandemic, this simply is no longer the case. As you operate in a networked world, we are connected far more than ever before. This isn't just due to technological advancement; with ever-growing populations, we are more and more affected by an array of interconnected, wicked social, economic, and environmental challenges. We are affected by ripples outside of our own sphere more than ever. There are always flow-on effects. And they have implications with respect to institutional trust.

Have We Reached Peak Trust?

Trust is just so important to society. It is equally important in government as it is in the private sector and other institutions. Trust is one of our most important currencies. Zak (2019) observed that trust is *the* enabler of global business and the infinite number of market transactions that take place, daily. Trust in government is vital for politicians to not only be re-elected but also deliver their policies. For organizational leaders, irrespective of the sector that they work in, trust is necessary if they are to:

- Attract and retain staff
- Ensure that an organization successfully creates the value it is meant to in line with its purpose, vision, and strategy
- Protect brand or reputation or, on the flip side, prevent or reduce disruptions stemming from stakeholder outrage
- Maintain high productivity from an engaged workforce

The list of reasons why trust is so vital for leaders to be effective and successful is long—particularly in an era where leaders are being scrutinized like never before.

Now, if you were to consider a previous discussion about the history of leadership and the heroic leader, in years gone by trust in such people would have come automatically. *No one* confronted the heroic leader. We simply followed their command without question.

Likewise, through the years, the dominating structures in society were not questioned. Our institutions and corporations were revered. We categorically trusted what they were doing on our behalf. We trusted that they had the expertise and the answers to our daily problems—and opportunities. They took care of *us*. For many years, this served us well.

Yet, trust is no longer a given. Edelman's Trust Barometer has bluntly observed that trust is in crisis in recent years across many Western nations and their institutions. But trust also struggles in institutions in some non-Western nations. There are many reasons including the momentous external changes that I described early on. Yet, it also includes the following:

- The changes that are being observed in cultural values across societies
- The problematic ways in which institutions respond to the change
- At a macro- and micro-level, the deep impacts that institutional decision making has had on the well-being of people within society

Let's talk about each of these.

More Sophisticated, Educated, and Sophisticated Than Ever Before

While I don't deny the challenges that we face, nevertheless, over the past few hundred years there have been overwhelming improvements, globally, in the lives of people. Within a generation, over one billion people have been lifted out of extreme poverty (World Bank 2018). One billion! Quite rightly, this is recognized as an extraordinary achievement.

There have been associated worldwide seismic improvements in health, life expectancy, and education. These improvements have also created the conditions for people to think about more than basic needs such as shelter, water, food, safety, and a job. Tibbs (2011) observed that these developmental improvements have created a springboard for a transformation of personal focus. Instead of people having to worry about those basic needs, they are now in a position where they can consider higher needs; they can think about what they would like the world to look like, shifting social values on a *massive* scale.

This has serious implications for seismic change, particularly with respect to regenerating lives, livelihoods, and the planet through a more regenerative mindset. Paul Ray and Sherry Ruth Anderson identified a significant cohort among the general populace with these values whom they labeled *Cultural Creatives*. This cohort questions the dominating worldviews and assumptions underlying our current systems. They expect a more balanced, more holistic approach to lives, livelihoods, and the planet rather than a focus solely on the stereotypical narrative of "fueling the economy, irrespective of the side effects." These issues gained much attention throughout the pandemic when many commentators argued for a reset of economies and the wider societal systems. Many have reflected on just what is important.

There is one point that I really want to emphasize. This segment of people—or tribe—is not small and cannot be ignored. According to Tibbs (2011), who reviewed an array of long-term studies concerning these changes in values, we have neared or crossed a tipping point at which a new cultural worldview is building toward dominance. This has been confirmed by futurist David Houle (2022) who forecasts that this global consciousness will decisively emerge in the second half of the 2020s. Across these various reviewed studies, the shifts do not appear to be limited solely to rich, developed countries but are evident across the world. This has massive implications for organizations, particularly when considered in tandem with the declining trust in our institutions, as observed over many years by Edelman.

This "great turning" may be a challenge to accept. Nevertheless, I want to emphasize how I see this all the time in my work—changes within society and changes in our views of institutions from those dominant even 10 years ago. I want to connect it with some other points to strengthen my case that systemic change has arrived and is something that you and other leaders will need to deal with, authentically, if your organizations are to thrive. And, as I write that, I realize it is easier for me to say than for you to do. But, as Elkington (2020) observed, the opportunities for all sectors in an age of uncertainty are just too appealing.

The first connection that I want to link with values changing substantially *across* societies is the previously introduced TIMN framework of Ronfeldt. He observes that as we shift toward a more networked world, power and influence shift to actors who are skilled or adept at developing multiorganizational networks in contexts where networks are the appropriate form of organization. Of warning to institutional leaders, Ronfeldt notes that not only are these networked organizations gaining strength relative to other forms, but that they are making life very difficult for traditional hierarchies with respect to maintaining their relevance. I see this time and time again: your stakeholders are becoming more sophisticated, educated, and coordinated than ever before, working in their networks with great agility. Institutions are struggling to adapt in response.

Consequently, I am arguing that the dominating worldviews and structures within societies are being questioned and eroded. While the record of 20th-century-style organizations and institutions adapting is scant, diminishing trust has profound consequences not only for their brand or reputation but also their productivity, innovation ... and even viability.

But the Institutions, They Ain't A-Changing

Questioning of how the system and organizations provide value and whether they can adapt isn't new. In that ground-breaking Brundtland Report, it was observed that the social, economic, and environmental sustainability challenges faced across the world "pose problems for institutions, national, and international." The report explained that because institutions were created to have a narrow focus and compartmentalized concerns, they are independent and fragmented, so unable to respond to the speed of global changes or to take a more integrated approach in dealing with sustainable development. You may recall that Bennis and Nanus were in agreement with how institutions were responding (at about the same time as the Brundtland Report was being developed), noting that there was "... a kind of plodding pandemonium" in place where institutions have been nothing but "rigid, slothful."

The Brundtland Report states that institutions have to evolve themselves, if these interdependent and integrated sustainability challenges were to be successfully confronted. Decisions regarding natural resources or social issues *should not* be siloed from decision making on economic and commercial issues. Emphatically, "The real world of interlocked economic and ecological systems will not change; the policies and institutions concerned must." The Brundtland Report (1987) made clear that urgency in our efforts is required: "The next few decades are crucial. The time has come to break out of past patterns. Attempts to maintain social and ecological stability through old approaches to development and environmental protection will increase instability."

That was 30 plus years ago.

It must be acknowledged that the narrative around the heroic leader and the way organizations have traditionally been led, with respect to transformative issues, has not been appropriate for decades. Worldviews haven't been questioned or adapted—nor kept up. While executive and emerging leaders are, broadly speaking, exceptional at solving linear problems, Rittel and Webber (1973) observed the *emergence* of wicked—or nonlinear—problems in the early 1970s. Even then, these complex challenges required a different, more collaborative, and empathetic means to deal with them.

Nevertheless, some commentators including Mukherjee (2016) and Holt, Macques, Hu, and Wood (2017) believe that leaders have failed their institutions. Leadership is often accused of outrageous behavior including greed, ego, lack of empathy, and exhibitionism. As examples, millions of Wells Fargo Bank's customer accounts were opened fraudulently to boost sales peoples' commissions, News Corp editors illegally hacked phones, and Volkswagen falsified emissions data on its diesel engines. It is easy to appreciate the adverse ramifications that this has for trust. Holt et al. (2017) offer a lengthy list of unethical laggards.

Commentators have proposed several reasons for this. Interestingly, Mukherjee (2016) notes that of great concern is the belief by many leaders that they can continue to run successful organizations employing 20th-century management thinking while in a much more volatile, interdependent, and fast-paced 21st century. Bennis and Nanus (1985) go much further, with respect to the complexity and uncertainty now faced, arguing that leaders lack the capabilities and emotional intelligence required to solve our wicked challenges. As the connections between organizations and society continue to grow, there are significant consequences to lives, livelihoods, and the well-being of the planet from organizational leaders who continue to be "ignorant and out of touch, insensitive, and unresponsive." Even worse, claim Bennis and Nanus (1985), too many leaders either hastily created solutions or did nothing, further exacerbating the problems faced.

There was a time in our social evolution when our institutions and the market were the most effective and efficient means by which to tackle our social, economic, and environmental issues. The challenges that we faced were linear in their resolution and our heroic leaders were highly competent at meeting them.

But we have been moving quickly into a more complex, networked world where change is no longer always linear. It's messy and exponential. And rather than having a society that is unquestioning of leaders, this networked world has connected people to information and each other in a way that amazes me. I see just how sophisticated, educated, and coordinated people are now in relation to the situations that they face.

Subsequently, our dominant worldviews and structures are now being actively questioned not only for their relevance but also for their performance and even their value or worth to society. This has ramifications for trust in our organizations and institutions, and therefore poses real threats to organizational reputation and brand for the many laggards.

Perceived Consequences

In an era where there is often news about the decline in lives, livelihoods, and the planet, I really want to emphasize that I appreciate the size of the challenge that leaders—from the C-suite or senior executives through to emerging talent—are being forced to grapple with regarding momentous and often downright hostile change simply to maintain the viability of their organizations. There must be times when you feel like you're a punching bag.

It is important, however, to consider how unresponsive, insensitive, siloed thinking that is perceived to be prevalent within organizations (as referred to by Bennis and Nanus 1985) affects your stakeholders. It's not good! And they certainly do not respond well to behaviors and language that reflects a worldview of "we know what's best for you." It is also important to consider what this means for trust and how it potentially reinforces a vicious circle for organizations with respect to their overall trustworthiness and reputation.

It is important to acknowledge that poor, dominating behavior from leaders toward stakeholders does not simply have short-term consequences. When someone feels they are having inappropriate values imposed upon them, then the consequences can be profoundly adverse and long term.

Zak (2019) provides a fascinating account of the neurological impacts of this common mindset and behavior from leaders. When an organizational leader mistreats stakeholders, internal and/or external, not only does this result in demotivation, but it also creates lasting hurt. This rejection, processed in our brains' pain matrix, establishes a signature to the social pain that lasts even longer than physical pain. This reduces the individual's desire to want to work with such a leader (or organization), reducing engagement and impacting productivity.

Exacerbating attitudes toward institutions and the value that they create is how change is characterized, especially in a world that is increasingly VUCA. Change associated with say technology or what we are experiencing with respect to the storm we face has an obvious S curve. As the change starts slowly, it may not be apparent to leaders or may be normalized as being nothing out of the ordinary. Accordingly, leaders don't act. However, the speed of change then grows at a steep rate (Tibbs 2011). All the while, stakeholders are increasingly frustrated because leaders still haven't adapted and accepted that there is now an urgent need to act. Worldviews are slow to evolve. Subsequently, what I see are members within the wider society who feel like they are being treated insensitively by institutional leaders, while gaining no committed response or acknowledgment concerning the seismic changes that worry, stress, or sadden them. How would being treated that way make you feel?

I ask you to keep that in mind when I shift back to discussing the institutional wide issues identified annually during the Edelman Trust Barometer (Edelman 2022). Ultimately, and worryingly, the Barometer continues to identify that there is a belief, particularly in the West (though not limited to there), that the system is failing and that leadership is failing across the board. Trust in authoritative institutions over the last 10 years, for example, has been reflected as being "in crisis"; that "business must partner with government to regain trust"; and that there is a "crisis in leadership."

If we dive down a little deeper, the Barometer—which surveys people in 28 countries—makes for increasingly uncomfortable reading with respect to how our institutions are faring with respect to affecting lives, livelihoods, and the planet, noting, for example:

- There is a strong belief that societal leaders are not trusted to do what is right and suspected of lying. Governments, for example, are seen as being unable to solve societal problems.
- Institutions are failing to address existential challenges. Societal fears are on the rise with respect to job security, climate change, cyberattack, losing freedoms, and racism.
- Capitalism as it stands today does more harm than good.
- Restoring trust is key to societal stability.
- There is strong belief that CEOs must lead on societal issues.

This distress in many societies can be associated with the concept of solastalgia, a form of emotional or existential distress caused by environmental change (Albrecht, Sartore, Connor, Higginbotham, Freeman, Kelly, Stain, Tonna, and Pollard 2007). This distress is directly related to people's home or community environment, which they place great importance on, and a belief that a connection to *home* has been violated (often by the imposition of unwanted development or government policies).

Indeed, their sense of place, their identity, physical and mental health, and general well-being are all challenged by unwelcome change—and exacerbated by a sense of powerlessness or lack of control over an unfolding monumental change process.

I respect that you may feel that these are simply peoples' perceptions. But, their perceptions are their reality. In fact, on reflection, I realize that simply talking about mental distress and trust—or the lack thereof—may not be strong enough language to express what implications this lack of adaptability and commitment in leadership to lives, livelihoods, and the planet can have for you and your organization. From my experience, when a stakeholder group and regional or local community have had enough, it can be shockingly destructive.

A Proliferation of Outrage

If this section hasn't made you feel uncomfortable yet about what organizations and institutions are exposed to due to how people perceive that lives, livelihoods, and the planet have been adversely impacted and ignored, then contemplate this: if your organization hasn't experienced outrage from key stakeholders yet, then you should prepare for it. In an era of increasing outrage, the chance that it will happen is significant and cannot be ignored. Outrage that doesn't take days but often months or years for organizations to remove themselves from; outrage that is costly, emotionally, and physically, creating delays in meeting work milestones and attracting media attention that, in turn, generates adverse attention from shareholders, government, the wider community, and other key stakeholders. Repeatedly, I see this, and it becomes self-perpetuating.

Even without the presence of your organization or government agency felt in a community or region, conflict and trauma can often *already* be present. And *imposing* a way forward on the affected, as has been customary, no longer has a high potential to work. This was driven home to me when I met the three Co-Directors of EcoPeace Middle East (ME).

The organization is an inspiring not-for-profit, championing a collaborative approach to protecting the region's shared environmental heritage. That's not easy in the best of situations. But in the Middle East? Bringing together Israeli, Jordanian, and Palestinian environmentalists, the organization is tackling the global water–energy nexus. By doing so, they are working toward a truly bold vision of a sustainable, prosperous, and peaceful Middle East (https://ecopeaceme.org/). If anyone is going to be successful in this context, it is got to be Israeli Gidon Bromberg, Jordanian Yana Abu Taleb, and Palestinian Nada Majdalani.

When I had the opportunity to talk to the three of them, together, I was struck by the genuine affection they had for one another. Smiles lit up each of their faces when seeing the other, recognizing the humanity in one another. An Israeli, a Jordanian, and a Palestinian enjoying being in each other's company? From my outsider's perspective, this was remarkable.

Yet, in their quest to champion the sustainable co-management of the Jordan River, individually, they've had to "push back" against the historical and powerful stories they have been fed about the "other." They are mindful of how their behavior and dominant worldviews could reinforce that which is embedded in the region rather than try to dilute it. While each of them is grounded in the reality of the generations' old hatred exhibited between the three nations, it must take significant emotional intelligence on their respective parts. Gidon, Yana, and Nada must always be mindful of their programs, their actions, and their messaging. All that they do has to be tactically well thought through. For the alternative is tremendously distressing; namely, stifled progress on increasing the efficient access to, and management of, freshwater in a region grappling with climate change and reduced rainfall.

A great lesson I could see from EcoPeace ME is that, culturally, it is an organization:

- That is aware of its place in the environment which it operates in.
- Has a deep appreciation of strategic issues like conflict in the region, the complex rights that are associated with access to freshwater, and the adverse implications of climate change and declining rainfall.
- Where success is only achieved through a deep respect toward their stakeholders and genuine collaborative involvement from leaders. This requires an acknowledgment that traditional leadership styles just won't work in their environment.

This is not to suggest that they expect the populace from each of the three nations to become warm friends; they are intensely realistic. They focus on understanding and managing the primary objectives for the governments and people that can be delivered through improved access to freshwater, be that water security or peaceful cooperation. Working collaboratively and cooperatively with your key stakeholders is vital for your organization's success.

We will hear from Gidon, Yana, and Nada in greater detail in Chapter 6 as there is much to learn from their collaborative style of leadership and their worldviews. However, while their inspiring story may seem extreme and removed from your situation, in a world that is increasingly VUCA, the chances of organizations being confronted by financially damaging conflict are high unless leaders acknowledge that the old ways of leading, thinking, doing, and being just no longer work. In the age of uncertainty, you will come across conflict and must deal with it, even when it's not of your organization's making. Yet, the practices and cultures of institutions can adversely impact a vast array of sustainability issues causing concerns and anger. Conflict often occurs because of parties pursuing incompatible goals. Specifically, the goals that institutions wish to progress can be incompatible with those of affected communities or societies with respect to the impact on lives, livelihoods, and the planet.

Wider conflict or outrage is also underpinned by the past weighing us down, shaping so much of our capacity to frame, interpret, and problem solve. Weights from the past which still create ripples or waves which include colonialism, tribalism, and patriarchy (Bussey 2006). These weights may be the reasons for trauma—referred to by Johan Galtung as "the wounds left from the past due to unresolved conflict." Where these "wounds" are left open and unhealed, people cannot be expected to always behave positively.

I am routinely surprised by how much energy an outraged person can draw on in order to fight "the big end of town" and create a win–loss situation, namely, a situation where they win at the expense of the organization, be that a corporation or government agency. Time and again, I have seen ordinary people take obsessive measures to the point of putting their own lives on hold—including work and family—to take ownership of their conflict.

Yet, too often, the stance from organizations toward the angry is that *they* are just unreasonable, and we will wait them out. Linked with the TIMN framework, this is reflective of a patriarchal worldview within many institutions and the mindset that "*we* know what is best for them." Conflict or outrage *will* remain and, in a networked world, will be acted upon by stakeholders. Even if you use force or legislation to remove opponents from your operations or a contested location, it can go underground but conflict and outrage will remain. And it will translate into continuing, negative media attention, protests, and violence, with impacts to the bottom line and impacts to staff engagement and retention—or worse.

Hope Springs Eternal

Nevertheless, there is hope. As Dr. Brundtland had been one of my inspirations for many years, while working previously in environmental management and then sustainability, I dearly wanted to find out her thoughts on this. Having been in office for three terms into the 1990s, followed by senior roles in the UN and World Health Organization, she is *still* proactively—and heavily—involved in efforts to improve lives, livelihoods, and the planet. Yet, she very kindly gave time to share some insights with me.

I wanted to learn what her views were on the Brundtland Report quoted above. For someone so heavily involved at the highest levels on these matters, I thought it would be only too natural for her to feel pessimistic. But I was mistaken.

"Yes, there are still limitations of the kind reflected upon here (in the Report)," she observed. "However, several new institutions, alliances, initiatives and not least international agreements have seen the light of day. They do illustrate the perceived limitations and the need to create a new basis for global cooperation to secure common goals."

The eye-opener for me was a realization that, through time, there certainly has been important progress made, even when it comes to action on climate change. "A tax on carbon dioxide emissions is now in place in a quarter of our countries, something unthinkable a decade ago."

While this gave me hope, I was mindful of those leaders who are well-meaning but don't know where to start with respect to confronting the storm or alternatively, the laggards who just won't accept that the storm is already here. What did she believe, with respect to the "old ways" or worldviews, is holding leaders back?

"Awareness that important initiatives for change will not be popular, at least short term, fear of opposition and losing political/popular support is the most obvious reason. Leaders need to rise up and go beyond short-term security and do what is right for coming generations."

Whether your organization is proactive or is dragged into accepting the change, excellent communication will be required to make the case to stakeholders, internal and external, as to why a shift in direction is required.

Dr. Brundtland then surprised me again. I asked her how she would motivate leaders, or create readiness, to instigate the changes necessary in response to what we are experiencing. She responded, "I would give them examples of policies that have been implemented and have led to both positive effects and increased respect for the forces and leaders behind radical change." It was quite succinct! And yet, it was these last two words—"radical change" highlighted what leaders now face. Incrementalism is no longer an effective approach; leaders need to be bold in their thinking and actions in the face of disruption.

One more thing about that concise sentence of Dr. Brundtland's regarding providing leaders with examples that have been implemented and which have led to positive effects and increased outcomes. I have felt compelled to share with you the stories of the leaders that I have interviewed about what the storm looks like to them. I need to convey a sense of urgency. And yet, I also want you to take away their insights, examples, and stories of hope.

It is time for organizations and their leaders to acknowledge the glorious past that they long for—where their efforts and goals weren't questioned or scrutinized—because those days have now passed. And it is time to meaningfully and strategically confront the storm of social, economic, and environmental upheaval that is already here. As you are about to hear, the resulting opportunities are just too compelling as is the breadth of strategic benefits that can be leveraged by organizations. For organizations to remain viable and thrive with certainty, a different way of thinking, connecting, doing, and understanding of is critical.

There is no longer time to wait.

Reflections

What do you want your organization's reputation to look like or to be perceived? What should the organization and your leadership be remembered for?

Is dealing with wicked problems a core competence within your organization?

What *genuine* contributions would your key stakeholders perceive your organization has made to improving lives and livelihoods and regenerating the planet?

If you have led your organization during a time that it was subjected to stakeholder outrage, what behavior was exhibited by you or your staff toward the outraged "other"?

If you *had to* lead your organization while it was subjected to stakeholder outrage, what would you do? What behaviors would be required?

Dr. Brundtland shared her thoughts on what is holding leaders back with respect to regenerating lives, livelihoods, and the planet. What do you think is holding leaders back?

– CHAPTER 4 –

CONFRONTING

THE STORM

Future generations will judge us not by what we say,
but what we do.

Ellen Johnson Sirleaf

Confronting the Storm

Leaders do not need to adapt to a changing world simply because it's the nice or moral thing to do. However, I am saying that leaders need to adapt to a changing world (and economy) because we face significant challenges that could become significant *opportunities.* As the pandemic has highlighted, we need to be adaptable to manage new formidable, strategic risks. In the age of uncertainty, these can leave our organizations exposed and prone to fragility.

Confronting Leadership

We have been poor at adapting to this suite of momentous changes. The story that we work to just no longer stands up to scrutiny; we are leaving a crescendo of interconnected crises placing us on a collision course with systemic collapse that threaten the viability, profit, and reputations of our institutions not to mention the impact on society and the planet (Fullerton 2015; Elkington 2020). To emphasize what this point in time looks like, I emphatically wanted to share with you Houle's (2022) observation that, "the new and future realities are rushing in everywhere one looks …. The old holds on, but is gasping and failing." Time is up.

The thinking by leaders, broadly, and the story of leadership has simply not kept up. The mechanistic view toward these challenges has not served us well; instead, what we face in terms of interconnected social, environmental, and economic forces, coupled with burgeoning human populations, will prompt a growing array of gradual than sudden breeches of what we take for granted as normality. These problems are no longer isolated points, but rather nodes in an interdependent network that is conveying grave concern as, associated with this, will be the creation of new types of wicked and even super wicked problems (Elkington 2020; Gibbons 2020; UNDP 2020). And the impact will be seismic. While "legacy thinking and institutions from the past are still in place, they are crumbling and collapsing" (Houle 2022). We can no longer afford to keep working hard just to maintain business as usual.

So, we may continue having dialogue about growth versus degrowth, generating resistance and argument. We need to tackle the root causes of "(un)sustainability" and take a more holistic, cooperative, and ambitious approach to what we are facing. We need to change the *characteristics* of growth. We need exponentially *less* of the degenerative forms of capitalism and exponentially *more* of the increasingly resilient forms (Elkington 2020; Gibbons 2020).

Therefore, to regenerate our lives, livelihoods, and the planet, we need to move toward a regenerative way of thinking and leadership.

Regenerating Hope

These challenges can be met and used for advantage if we stop treating these issues, reflective of the storm, as altruistic "nice to haves" through our awkwardly bolted-on, unsuccessful, sustainability, or corporate social responsibility programs or through superficial, short-term, government policies. Instead, we need to focus on those issues of relevance (to a specific organization and its stakeholders) and treat them as issues that are strategically *critical* to the success of leaders and their organizations and therefore, place them front and center.

Rather than focusing on triple bottom line or CSR approaches, many organizations are working toward an integrated bottom line. That means efforts need to traverse vision, strategy, new products, processes, and supply chain integration. That integration has significant benefits for the organization. Indeed, there is anecdotal evidence that those organizations that are acknowledged as leaders in social and environmental issues— those organizations that are integrated—perform better than nonintegrated organizations (Sroufe 2017).

This needs to call on reasoning from leaders that is holistic in nature, embracing the notion that the economy—and politics—is not disconnected from social or environmental issues. Yet, the thinking should go further than this. A regenerative mindset or worldview is one that appreciates that the organization cannot deplete or pollute to the detriment of the immediate and wider surrounds. It goes beyond organizations' sustainability efforts, which focus on reducing the environmental and social impacts to maintain business as usual. Rather, it is about better understanding the relationship with the system within which your organization finds itself located in; the mindset should facilitate our social and ecological systems fulfilling the overall potential of the place, community, organization, or leaders to thrive (Elkington 2020; Gibbons 2020; Hahn and Tampe 2021).

This is not just an opportunity for corporations. So, too, governments, government agencies, and not-for-profits have a role to play in enabling lives, livelihoods, and the planet to flourish. It also needs social mobilization from the bottom-up involving your stakeholders (UNDP 2020). That takes different approaches to the status quo.

Regenerating Opportunities

I haven't really quantified the opportunities from confronting the status quo. You may feel that such a concept of regeneration is going way too far, that industry would suffer if cultural values were to change to this extent. What would this mean for jobs? And considering how our approaches have served us well for generations, just why should we change?

Elkington (2020) observed that meeting the UN Sustainable Development Goals in just 4 out of 60 sectors alone (namely, food and agriculture, cities, energy and material, and health and well-being) could open astonishing market opportunities worth up to U.S.$12 trillion per year by the early 2030s. Furthermore, Garrido, Fazekas, Pollitt, Smith, Berg von Linde, McGregor, and Westphal (2018) observe that while business as usual growth could mean over 140 million climate migrants by 2050, in comparison, transitioning to a low-carbon, sustainable growth path could deliver a direct economic gain of U.S.$26 trillion through to 2030. What other opportunities are possible?

There are not just positive financial outcomes to be attained. For government and nongovernment agencies, there are significant benefits to be had, from a holistic perspective. Just think about enhanced reputation among a deeply cynical and distrustful society, enhanced productivity, and engagement from staff who see genuine approaches taken to resolve what we face, to name just a few.

This means breaking out of "incrementalism at all costs" thinking and the desire to innovate only to maintain business as usual. As David from LALA observed, from scarcity, we can advance toward abundance.

"There's Just Great Opportunities to Step Up"

Many organizations may not be able to head straight to regenerative services or products; I get this. But, to give society and your organization enough time to deal with the storm, it means putting in place practices that are at least more restorative than a focus on meeting the barest of legislated minimums or sustainability programs that are all about the marketing opportunities. Leaders need to be strategic, committed, and proactive.

Remember David from LALA's provocative challenge? The ability for your organization to thrive is in your hands. This is available to leaders with an open commitment to confronting the dominating worldviews that have brought us here. How strategic your organization is with respect to confronting the storm in the context of a world that is experiencing far-reaching and turbulent change will also make for astute risk management in the 21st century.

Don't take my word for it. Let's hear from the passionate Daniel Epstein, CEO of Unreasonable Group. Based in Colorado, he was named by *Fortune* magazine as one of the world's 50 greatest leaders, also receiving the prestigious "Entrepreneur of the World" award, along with Richard Branson and former Liberian President Ellen Johnson Sirleaf at the Global Entrepreneurship Forum. Daniel is an innovative thinker, whose views are worthwhile reflecting on when it comes to adopting the kind of big picture leadership that we now need.

It was fascinating when I had the opportunity to catch up with Daniel and Milena Stojceska, Unreasonable Group's Manager, Investor Experience, and learn about the opportunities open to them from being strategic, committed, and proactive.

Daniel started our conversation by sharing his impatience when it comes to putting a dent in the world's biggest challenges. He observed that "there's more people alive today who don't have access to electricity than when Thomas Edison turned on the first light bulb. A population of about 1.3 to 1.4 billion people. So, if you don't have access to electricity, what do you do? You turn to burning wood, so you tear down forests. Or you have kerosene if you're burning kerosene lanterns like about a billion people do, today … for lighting. That's the equivalent of every woman, man and child in each household smoking two packs of cigarettes a day. We need to change that dynamic as fast as possible. And we have over 760 million people who can't read a sentence who are adults. I think that's a shocking reality. What about recidivism rates out of prison systems with the US having 80% recidivism? Or talk about climate change. It's not climate change—it's a climate crisis with about 17 million climate refugees, right now. If we're not impatient about solving these problems, they're only going to get worse. It's not like if we continue with the status quo that it will just remain as bad as things currently are; things are only going to get worse."

It kind of leaves you breathless, right? Yet, what he sees are so many market opportunities.

It's interesting to note that Daniel was quite reflective, admitting that he wasn't always like this. He didn't start Unreasonable or affiliated companies out of a feeling of obligation or responsibility. Instead, he had an epiphany one night. When he was thinking about entrepreneurs and their designed solutions to problems, he decided that he was only going to work on problems that were worthy of his life's work. "Why not pick a problem worth solving? It's just more compelling, it's just more exciting. For me, it was more the opportunity and realization that it's possible to run companies that exist for social and environmental purpose. It got me excited more so with an awareness of how sticky these global challenges are and that we needed to do something about them."

Just as Elkington observed, the opportunities for Unreasonable have been truly significant.

Milena agreed. "I think there's just such great opportunities for companies to finally step up. There's never been a more important time for business to do so and there's never been a better time for investors to consider that environmental, social, and governance is outperforming mainstream funds. When you prioritize ESG (environmental, social, and governance) issues, you're going to get the return and that trend is only going to continue. It's a brilliant intersection of profit and purpose."

Interestingly, Daniel is now seeing the changes required in societal thinking to confront the storm come to fruition in the business world. "I think the world was much more bifurcated even five years ago in terms of 'you do well and then you do good', right? I think now, there's been this transformation where we've seen a lot of people say, 'well hang on, you could actually do well *and* do good at the same time'. If you want to maximize the amount of financial return that you have, then you need to maximize the amount of good that you're creating in the world. You need to maximize both simultaneously. My real belief is that the future titans of industry can be the companies solving the world's hardest problems because they're creating more value and the markets are recognizing that. And that shows up through the stories of our companies. We support just over 300 growth-stage CEOs and their companies and over the last couple of years, they've raised about U.S.$7 billion. Much more important is that these companies have measurably impacted the lives of over 700 million people around the world and these companies are the proof that they are the trend setters." He could have listed about 300 examples. It was absolutely amazing to listen to.

"We" Over "I"

Hopefully, what I have been able to explain in the preceding chapters is that the change we are seeing has created a cumulative, interconnected force. A nonmarket force, in the traditional sense, that inevitably pulls us toward a future that has seismic implications for society, its institutions, and the economy, alike. Daniel, intriguingly, identified these challenges as being market failures that we, importantly, can treat as market opportunities.

Now, just as a good organizational strategy has the right "fit" with the internal and external environment within which it operates, so too leadership must adapt and have the right fit with the change that has occurred. When the push comes from numerous social, economic, and environmental forces of sizeable scale and consequence, then the heroic leader or the command-and-control leader just cannot be relied upon to successfully find a way forward.

Such leadership was brilliant during times of stability and for solving linear problems. In this era where our problems are messy or nonlinear, these styles of leadership are inappropriate. Rather, a collective form of leadership is categorically required if organizations are to improve or protect their brand, reputation, productivity, and viability. We need leaders who are compelled by something other than accumulating personal power and status because organizations will suffer from this individualistic mindset. We need leaders who have transcended the egocentric and instead, passionately want to develop leaders, within and without, developing them in such a way that they are equipped and enabled to think strategically and act decisively. The storm requires an array of leaders in each organization with a diversity of perspectives to deal with the complexities.

Daniel believed that the next generation of entrepreneurs is going to look remarkably different from those trained in business schools in the 20th century. "With people talking about competitive advantage, I think that businesses that are going to win are going to be those that understand collaborative advantage and focus on that instead. When we do selection processes for those start-ups that we may work with, we look at the characteristics of the CEOs. What we are looking for is a paradoxical blend of confidence and humility in leaders. They believe that they can actually make a real difference in the world for the better, but they have enough humility to acknowledge that the greatness of what they achieve will be through the greatness of their teams." The humility is the aspect that provides the focus on the collaborative advantage.

Shared leadership on our key strategic challenges will be vital as we observe that organizations are being tested like never before while operating in an increasingly VUCA world. Without committing to a shift, the resulting brittleness within organizations will spell commercial and/or reputational disaster—and will happen sooner rather than later.

Vulnerability to the "Kodak Moment"

I am going to come back to that conversation about what I think the required shift in leadership styles needs to look like. No leader wants to be known as the one who was responsible for their organization having a "Kodak moment." You've heard the story, right? How Kodak fell by the wayside when photography transformed from film to digital? Kodak's leaders downplayed the emerging transformation, believing that the corporation's glorious past would continue. Disruption really can be a killer.

However, the impacts now being observed with respect to long-term organizational viability are downright shocking. Having undertaken a detailed investigation of U.S. public companies, Reeves, Levin, and Ueda (2016) identified that companies of all shapes, sizes, and sectors are disappearing faster and dying younger than ever before. Of the 30,000 public companies whose longevity they investigated over a 50-year period, the delisting rate of companies is now *six times* what it was 40 years ago. It is reasonable to assume that this "rate of extinction" has been significantly magnified by the pandemic.

This confirms my argument that organizations and their inherent leadership style too often have a poor "fit" with the momentous change occurring within their environment. Organizations have failed to adapt not only to change in general but also to the change we are seeing with respect to globally interconnected trends around the storm.

On reflection, I hope that the descriptions I've given to this point adequately communicate the kind of disruption anticipated—the scale, frequency, and consequences. While the pandemic awoke peoples' imaginations to potential disruption, I'm not sure that leaders appreciate that even this perspective is simplistic. What do you think? Perhaps, the pandemic could have been viewed as just one layer of the seismic challenges we now face, each of which has the potential to contribute to seismic cumulative disruption.

Regenerating Leadership

This chapter and the book content in general aren't about the transactional leader focused on the day-to-day operations of an organization. The focus here is on the strategic leader, like you, who is lying awake at night thinking about the risk of a Kodak moment and/or because of your passion to lead something of greater meaning.

You may be wondering why I am focusing on you? Well, it is you who plays a key role in shaping cultures; it's you who can determine if staff and stakeholders are engaged; you are the one with the power to develop and enable more leaders to confront the storm.

To transcend current sustainability practices, manage these strategic social, economic, and environmental risks, and shift toward a more regenerative mindset, we need to transcend traditional leadership practices. In a world where there is a commercial, governance, and reputational need for committed action from leaders, it comes at a time where the gap between what is needed and what we currently have in place has never been wider.

We need to move to a more inclusive, holistic, and more supportive form of leadership that enables diverse and collective effort. This "servant-style" of leadership will enable organizational leaders and their influential stakeholders to be better informed, make better decisions, and deal more strategically and holistically with what we face. It will require a fundamental paradigm shift for many leaders but, for the sake of the viability, reputation, and success of your organization, there is no alternative.

Robert Greenleaf coined "servant leadership," recognizing that there were contexts where leaders need to go "beyond one's self-interest," that "It begins with the natural feeling that one wants to serve, to serve first. Then conscious choice brings one to aspire to lead" (Greenleaf 1970). Interestingly, research has shown that the notion of putting others first is a leadership style that spans diverse cultures (Pekerti and Sendjaya 2010).

To me, servant leadership implies a different mentality to what I often see; it implies a shift from the individualistic focus on self to a collective focus, serving and supporting staff, other stakeholders, society, and the planet, in general. What about you?

In response to that notable decline in trust that I discussed with you previously is a growing expectation that leaders will focus not only on shareholders and staff but other human and biological stakeholders as well and do so in a transparent and ethical manner. Leadership approaches that focus on and authentically support "the other" are being increasingly valued; by focusing on what is best for the "other," the servant leader consequently obtains what is best for the organization (Winston and Fields 2015; Kiker, Callahan, and Kiker 2019).

"Our fundamental belief in the Unreasonable Group," observed Daniel, "is that the 'we is greater than I' principle is definitely a foundational value for us. There's no panacea solution for any global issue whether social or environmental. As the Nobel Peace Prize winner Muhammad Yunus said, 'there's enough poverty in the world for all of us'. We don't need to be competitive to try to solve these market failures and I would say that for issues around health care, education, poverty alleviation, social and environmental justice, environmental degradation, and species extinction; there's enough of that to go around. The only way we're going to see a better future is if we can collaborate towards it."

This can feel confronting, yet, when we look at leadership through the years, have the dominant heroic or command and control styles always seemed to make sense? Like so much that happens, the leadership that we have in place is built on a social construct. So much about it with respect to leadership and followership is an illusion, created by our traditional stories, experiences, and arguably, testosterone. Doesn't leadership need to adapt and be appropriate for the times and context faced? I want to make it clear that a regenerative mindset within organizations is not only achievable but also from a strategic, commercial, and reputational perspective is vital considering the big picture context that we find ourselves in.

The Framework: Transforming Leadership, Transcending Sustainability

From what I have been synthesizing from my research, my interviews, and my experience working with leaders over many years, strategically there are specific key behaviors and skills leaders require to successfully navigate their organizations through an increasingly VUCA context and to facilitate a more regenerative mindset when it comes to confronting the storm of social, economic, and environmental forces that we face (Figure 4.1).

As the Regenerating Leadership Framework implies, it is meant to be three dimensional, almost fluid in nature. My framework has a structure that highlights the chronological order to develop a strategic way forward—"connecting: co-creating with dignity" *and then* strategic delivery of this—"doing: embrace the storm." Yet, the framework also, by location, implies inputs to this—"thinking: better informed to transcend the unthinkable"—and importantly, the deeper, subconscious issues that underpin this, that we, as leaders, must reflect on—"becoming: understanding the other and ourselves" if we are to be successful at being regenerating leaders.

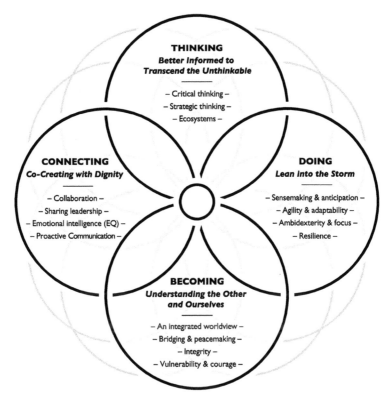

Figure 4.1 Regenerating leadership framework

It's nonlinear.

While for ease of reading, the key skills and behaviors have been "pigeon-holed" into one of the four lenses, you will realize as you read through the coming chapters that some of these key skills and behaviors could be just as relevant elsewhere in the framework.

Instead, the diagram intends to imply in its three-dimensional makeup that leaders, in working at new skills and behaviors, can come upon transitional states where they are simultaneously looking backward to what they are comfortable with, regarding their thinking and doing, while also looking forward to new ways unfolding. It is appreciated that such states of emergence, the "betwixt and between spaces and times," create ambiguity and "unknowing" for leaders as they are removed from their comfort zones and instead, find themselves grappling with "tensions, dislocations, and disruptions" (Orton and Withrow 2015). Have you felt that? I've certainly felt that discomfort! Most importantly, these encounters with self-doubts about what we've learned, or our worldviews are central to learning; once we grasp one new concept that creates epiphanies and takes us across the threshold, others come into realization, facilitating transformations (Hawkins and Edwards 2015). Transformations that will be vital in us will be successfully confronting the storm.

Each of these four lenses will be covered in greater detail in Chapters 5 to 8 with further questions for you so that your reflection can be tailored to your specific context. I do not expect you to feel immediately connected to all that is proposed here. So, I don't want to rush through these concepts. It's too important.

Reflections

Houle observed that "new and future realities are rushing in everywhere … the old (order) holds on, but is gasping and failing." Has that shown itself in your sector? If so, how?

What does growth look like at present within your industry or as supported by your government? As Gibbons observes, is it (un)sustainable?

Is incrementalism your organization's mantra when dealing with our wicked problems?

How could your organization experience disruption or its own "Kodak moment"? Is there the risk of organizational brittleness?

What could regenerative thinking look like for you?

Where have you seen leaders who mirrored Greenleaf's servant-style leaders who go "beyond one's self-interest"? What did that look like? How did it benefit others or an organization?

As a leader in this context faced, what do you think that you need to *be*?

– CHAPTER 5 –

THE GALES
HAVE ABATED

We don't see things as they are; we see them as we are.

Anais Nin

– CHAPTER 5 –

The Gales Have Abated

The first step of walking you through the framework—thinking—must seem so obvious to you. And yet, I'm still confident that we need to talk about it. You see, my experience has been that thinking is something that numerous leaders *unwittingly* struggle with. This has enormous ramifications with respect to how an organization confronts complexity as well as dealing with momentous and turbulent change—and ramifications for the organization, itself (Figure 5.1).

Figure 5.1 Thinking

Do we take thinking for granted? Is it something that is undertaken very instinctively?

Certainly, in years gone by, leaders were brilliant at instinctively making decisions with respect to linear-style problems. Yet, since we no longer live in a world where linear problems dominate our higher-level thinking, the thinking that leaders required in the past, often reductive in nature, to inform decision making may need to be condemned to the past. Remember that our deeper challenges and opportunities in an increasingly VUCA world are now messy and complex. So, the outcomes of dealing with messy problems with old-style thinking are also, well, messy. Indeed, as I implied previously, based on my interactions with organizations and how their stakeholders respond to old-style thinking, I cannot emphasize enough just how messy it can get!

Thinking: Better Informed to Transcend the Unthinkable

Trying to think *thoughtfully* and make decisions, with answers of real meaning to enhance or regenerate lives, livelihoods, and the planet, is always going to be a challenge.

Firstly, it can be challenging because of the complexity and the interconnectivity that exists within *and between* lives, livelihoods, and the planet. And I am not just talking about living in a networked world, although that certainly has a considerable bearing. We're also talking about the complexity inherent within ecosystems, natural and social. Contrary to some dominant worldviews, ecosystems aren't mechanistic like a car; you cannot pull them apart like a car, confident that when you "put it back together" again, it will work perfectly. There is a complexity and connectivity from a macro- to a micro-scale within ecosystems that we struggle to replicate. And an impact on part of an ecosystem, by nature, has positive or negative consequences for other parts. Some consequences may be foreseeable, and some won't be. Therefore, organizations must be quite considered in their thinking. A Western reductionist worldview of breaking things into their subunits will not always be effective.

Secondly, in an increasingly networked and uncertain world, we grapple with so much information being available as well as being confronted by different—indeed, polarizing—perspectives. Some information is accepted as being true, based on dominant worldviews and where we place value or emphasis. However, our blind spots cause us to accept some "facts" as being correct when they are merely perceptions. Furthermore, it is common for leaders to make decisions based on what they see "at the surface" with respect to sustainability and regeneration issues, rather than understanding the root causes of what they are witnessing. They don't examine the depths beneath. Suffice it to say, get things wrong and delivery of your vision, strategy, programs, or projects have a high chance of being unsuccessful, and in this age of uncertainty, may come at a price to the organization. And this is what happens repeatedly. When it comes to tackling our complex social, economic, and environmental challenges, it is extremely hard to find organizations from across industries or sectors that are delivering anything of note. And stakeholders see that for what it is.

An important first step to do something meaningful about contributing to lives, livelihoods, and regenerating of the planet is for leaders to appreciate that it is in their best interests to improve their capability to be adept and disciplined in their thinking. And the same applies to their staff too. We need organizations with critical and strategic thinkers to respond to an increasingly VUCA context. We must develop the ability to make sense of a world which is no longer full of black and white situations; but rather, it is full of grays. This will be confronting for many disciplines that have, historically, taken a simplified approach to weighing up decision making. It requires an openness to more holistic and integrated ways of thinking as well as an openness to different perspectives.

If we are to reflect on how we go about our thinking, I need to bring the wonderfully warm and humble Eva Karlsson into the conversation. As the CEO of the Swedish brand, Houdini Sportswear, Eva's strategic and critical thinking has been called on to make Houdini such a successful—and respected—brand. Houdini—and Eva—are genuine in their efforts to make a seismic difference; but more on that, shortly. Let's go back to that discussion about the validity of the old ways of thinking still being employed.

I had asked Eva about an observation of Houdini's that society needs to have a sense of urgency to break free from the status quo with respect to our thinking toward lives, livelihoods, and the planet. Deeply reflective, Eva noted that was written at a time when "the context that we were in felt like we were very much alone at looking at business and the degenerative practices that business has just taken for granted—not only a business as such, but also the system that we have to play within. These practices are valued and regulated by the system; that we can be proud of profits that are gained at the expense of others, be it ecosystems or people. That was nothing that people reflected on. It was just the way it was."

This mindset appears to be incomprehensible to Eva. "Regarding breaking free of that system, a lot of things we can change on our own, and some things we can persuade our partners out there to go along with us and change some of it. Then again, there's a lot of things that we just cannot do, because we're stuck in a system. And that to me is extremely frustrating. So, we've spent our time detangling where we can, and then changing where we can on our own. There's a lot of people that have awakened slightly, but I think we're at a crossroads. If this pandemic doesn't help us take the right direction, I don't know what will."

What do you think will be the appropriate conditions for us to shift? Milojević and Inayatullah (2021) observe that society has entered a highly uncertain and unpredictable period. Many will be tempted to go back to the world we knew, one where nature is still seen as an externality, and profit is the core focus of all activities; yet it is also an opportunity to create a different world and instigate structural change. This requires strategic thinking.

Strategic Thinking: It's Not About Wish Lists

Now, it can sometimes feel like everyone thinks that they are strategic or has a strategy of some kind. Yet, are they really strategies? Or are they often just wish lists or something like that, with little rhyme or reason to them? Do they seem a little unrealistic when it comes to what they hope to deliver? Perhaps you have seen that? In my opinion, this often comes down to an abject lack of strategic thinking in leaders.

Strategic thinking isn't easy to begin with when it comes to considering lives, livelihoods, and the planet. It takes more than a reliance on facts. There needs to be consideration of people and different perspectives;

dealing with this is certainly best viewed as an art and science (Yarger 2006). Yet, irrespective of the difficulties associated with strategic thinking, a key reason it is a challenge for many is simply that it is a capability many lack. And much has to do with the so-called leadership paradox.

It is often possible for people in technical roles, from junior to middle management level, to get by without developing this skill. This certainly includes those in sustainability or CSR management roles. Often, the work for juniors or the middle manager is project based, focusing on an important niche function within the organization. To succeed in these roles requires a focus to be placed on, for example, technical expertise, teamwork, initiative, project control, effective communication, and influencing skills. This all makes a lot of sense while people remain at those levels.

Troubles arise, subsequently, for many leaders and managers when they progress into senior roles based on the excellence that they exhibited in their technical roles yet have to tackle nonlinear issues and work through others. However, the skills that got them into leadership roles—the technical expertise—are what they wish to unwittingly maintain their emphasis and attention on, rather than be true strategic thinkers. Paradoxically, their technical expertise and excellence then becomes a hindrance.

A key clarification that I better make now is that strategic thinking *is different from* strategic planning, although both are important for strategic management of an organization as well as strategic leadership. They are distinct but interrelated and complementary thought processes (Heracleous 1998). While there is an array of definitions for strategic thinking (Heracleous 1998; Wright 2018), I really like Yarger's (2006) challenge that strategic thinking needs to be "considered from the perspective of systems within systems interacting in both linear and nonlinear ways." Certainly, with sustainability and regeneration issues, this is applicable, but it can be difficult to appreciate all nuances that are imaginable within a world of great complexity. I believe that Yarger's (2006) view implores strategic thinkers to metaphorically take a step back to understand not only bigger picture implications but also how the distinct parts of the systems are interconnected, thereby improving our holistic thinking. Hahn and Tampe (2021) refer to the "nestedness" of local issues or trends in a larger context so that small interventions can influence the health of the entire system or how changes in the larger ecosystem can have repercussions on resilience at a local level. Thus, rather than taking a reductive approach, strategic thinking "seeks to understand how the parts form the whole by looking at parts *and* relationships among them" (Yarger 2006).

That, right there, is a quote that I so strongly connected with. If leaders could understand that more focus needs to be placed on the interconnectivity of market and nonmarket issues, then I believe that they would be much better decision makers as a consequence.

Committed and Authentic

I have come across few people that seek to understand how the parts form the whole better than Eva. I really mean that. Houdini makes sustainable, outdoor clothing for adults through to kids. This is where its similarities to most of the global clothing brands end. Rather than disposing of excess material to landfills, sustainability truly is at the heart of the organization. There are two reasons why I love that.

The first is the circularity in their inputs and outputs that relates to a restorative manufacturing system. That is, 100 percent of what they use is now recycled, recyclable, renewable, or biodegradable; they even repair or rent out their clothing (https://houdinisportswear.com). These interlinked efforts go deeply against the grain of an industry that is highly fickle and disposes of last season's clothing with abandon. So much so that research has found that the average garment is worn somewhere between seven and ten times in the western world. That forces 150 billion clothing items to be made annually. Just think of the waste, not to mention that the apparel industry is the second-largest polluter of freshwater, globally! Instead, Houdini's efforts aim to reduce clothing consumption and wastage while increasing the usage and product life cycle (Shank and Bédat 2016; Housman 2020).

The second and arguably more important reason why I love this is that they don't try to place a slant or spin on their situation to make things look favorable when they have not achieved all that they intend to. They have mapped out to 2066 just what they believe they need to do to not only achieve zero waste but also become a positive and regenerative force in society and for the planet. You may remember previously when I referred to the planetary boundaries framework? Well, Eva and Houdini are thought to have undertaken the first such assessment for a business, providing them with the comprehensive information necessary for them to understand the parts and the whole and work toward a 2066 that looks like this:

"Decoupled from today's unsustainable societal system, Houdini together with likeminded, have cultivated a new societal system where nature, society, economy and technology work in harmony and life is flourishing" (Houdini 2021).

By seeing the parts and the whole, Eva and Houdini have, strategically, seen significant opportunities. "Yes, businesses have just been thinking in a linear way and not realizing that there's opportunity for us to cater to our customers and end users in a much, much stronger way," Eva noted. "And I think, what we mean moving from a transactional economy, with no real relations with stakeholders, we've moved it to work the relations economy. We believe that is the way to help each other care and evolve together. So, it really makes sense. And that way we can provide service and knowledge to our customers and end users in a way that seems very human. We can exceed customer expectations many times because, you know, that caring for users is very unusual. I guess that way, we exceed expectations and our ways of relating to our customers, and engaging with them, also usually exceeds expectations. Although it's only common sense, what we're doing," Eva modestly observed.

While it is all very well to focus on the need to develop strategic thinking capabilities in your organization, this won't matter if, in the increasingly VUCA world, the information you are calling on is of inadequate quality or insular in nature. Seeing internal and external environments as interconnected ecosystems goes a long way toward helping that.

It's All Ecosystems, Baby!

I want to briefly touch one more time on that definition from Yarger (2006) on strategic thinking, about understanding how the parts form the whole by looking at parts and relationships among them. For many leaders, used to linear-worlds and linear-world problems, this is tough to absorb. That is why I want to introduce viewing all a leader has to face in terms of ecosystems—because I believe that if you can visualize what you face as an ecosystem, you can go a long way to understanding your context, identifying where you may face challenges as well as anticipating the flow-on effects from your decisions, to name a few. It can help you to significantly improve your strategic thinking.

The term "ecosystems" has gained increasing prominence in the 21st century, extending beyond a focus on the natural environment to considering social, IT, and business ecosystems. For me, some commentators have not genuinely appreciated the full consequences of operating in ecosystems. One view is that operating in an ecosystem creates an expectation that within the supply chain, smaller organizations can succeed if they adhere to the rules and standards created by the "bigger fish" (Longobardi 2004). This is the patriarchal worldview that "we, the large organizations, know best." That level of closed thinking can create an array of problems as the strengths of the wider ecosystem are not appreciated—to the detriment of all concerned.

Let's visualize an ecosystem. What does it look like? Hmm. I'm not sure if this is going to be the greatest of visualizations or apt descriptions but think of a three-dimensional lattice; only think of the lattice as *not having* a definable central core to it. Can you see primary struts and support struts and nodes where the different types of struts meet? Hopefully, you are seeing something! Think of the nodes as representing say, your organization, other organizations, prominent individuals, communities, natural ecosystems, or nations. With that in mind as well as the strands that connect the nodes, I have always viewed this imaging as being tremendously helpful in considering the parts, the whole, and even how what may feel like your organization's world is in fact, a part of something even bigger. This is why I deliberately referred to a lattice with no definable central core to it—to get you thinking how your organization may hold a very random position in an ecosystem and does not have the power that may be appropriate if coming from a patriarchal mindset. System thinkers may wonder why I refer to this as ecosystem thinking and so they should. In this case, I want to try my best to facilitate you seeing the connections between your organization and the much *wider* world.

Ripples Have Consequences

There's one more consideration that I wanted to share with you here about the ramifications of existing in an ecosystem. Have you seen from a spider's perspective, how something touching one part of the web is sensed by the spider, even if it is on the other side of the web? It is interactive. It's continuous. It's everywhere (Gallis and Millar 2006). This emphasizes how leaders need to be able to think in such a way to appreciate how there can be ripples on another part of the ecosystem that have flow-on effects for your organization and for you. Greater—and holistic—awareness is required in the age of uncertainty.

In a networked world, decisions in one part of the ecosystem affect the other. Consequently, when it comes to the strategic, all our interventions and decisions matter. They have impact and—do not forget—unintended consequences. On the flip side, *hope* can be regenerated through small interventions that can positively influence the larger system. Herrero (2010), for example, notes that implementing a small set of chosen and defined behaviors can create significant and powerful change. This does not have to be driven top-down throughout an organization. Instead, leaders like you can tap into your "influencers." Unlike most nodes in your ecosystem, influencers are connected to other stakeholders by countless more strands than your average Joe or Josephine. When influencers adopt a unitary collective behavior, their influence on the organization's behalf can be profound. Critical considerations are vital.

Eva and Houdini have taken ecosystems thinking further than most companies, exploring how we can understand ecosystem processes, learn from them, and aim to integrate them into Houdini's work. "We truly have some kind of compelling vision in our mind. I don't see how anybody, whether it's a leader of a company or anyone else, cannot understand that we have to understand how we're impacting the planet, our only planet—this is our home! So, we need to understand these extremely complex systems. Of course, we don't even know everything about it. Far from it. But we know enough to design our ways of doing business in the best ways and at least reduce our harm."

I'm going to interrupt Eva there for a second. You may be thinking that she is *only* talking about ways to reduce social and environmental impacts or comply with legislation or reduce costs. It is certainly that, but it is so much more. By seeing people or the finite resources within the environment through a different lens, leaders can instigate regenerative practices within their organizations that benefit lives, livelihoods, and the planet, while also enhancing innovation, commercial opportunities, and better management of risks, to say the least. If you still haven't thought much about your organization's role in confronting the storm, you definitely might want to after this next bit from Eva.

"We can also find ways where we can partner up with nature. We have examples of that today, where we can see that there are actual technologies and ways of working to become a partner with nature, rather than this colonial way of looking at it as a resource that we are just constantly consuming. I guess that everybody knows that we're consuming everything that makes life worth living and makes life possible. So, all of us better look to that system and see how we can change. Because there's not going to be any resources and there's not going to be any customers and there's not going to be anything to build value from if we continue. I don't understand how one couldn't want to engage and learn more about that."

"By holding hands with Earth system scientists, we can explore how we're doing right now, but also 'what if we did that instead of this?' You start playing with it and start understanding how we can evolve from here, step by step. That's so exciting, so rewarding. And we want to make sure that we communicate that to the outside world, as well, because it's really important that everyone takes that wider perspective on things before they start moving in a new direction, creating maybe even more harm somewhere else."

Houdini has, consequently, been experiencing robust growth. The outdoor clothing industry is highly competitive with regular new entrants into the market and the risk of growing similarity in offerings. Yet, Houdini had consistently been obtaining 20 percent annual growth since 2014 (Holtström, Bjellerup, and Eriksson 2019). Doing good is indeed good for business.

By seeing the parts and the whole, Eva was philosophical and passionate about what Houdini is achieving. "I guess it's a mix of responsibility and opportunity. Staying with the problem is one thing but staying with the problem is not something that we like. We would rather move on to reimagining things, and then moving ahead in a new direction that seems smarter, not only for us and the planet, but also for our customers. I think we can find a win–win–win when we look at it appropriately. I guess conventional businesses just do what they've always been doing, not even exploring to find these new solutions. At the core, I guess, we realized just how many products were produced, that eventually had to become wasted, because they were designed in a poor way. That was a reality that we understood we had to get away from if we were to become part of the solution. How do we design a system where we all become caretakers of those resources rather than consumers? And that's why we started designing circular products and trying to mimic nature and extremely complex, perfectly functioning systems where everything flows and there are constant feedback loops. But yes, we can at least start getting to the point where we contribute rather than take."

Critical Thinking: Problematize Where You Place Meaning

This is a point in our conversation where I want to steer the conversation to the importance of questioning where we source information from in the first place, to be able to make the best decisions possible. I have noted that, when it comes to linear problem-solving, leaders could call on their experience or instinct. I've also alluded to where leaders may call on peers or direct-reports who all think in the same way—groupthink. Those means, quite simply, could worsen the situation when confronting the storm that we face.

In a nonlinear world, where we are exposed to volumes of information, it could be argued that we are almost fabricated to see the world in a particular way for several reasons.

Firstly, as we are exposed to so much information, our brains make the processing so efficient so that we see things in patterns. And, as discussed previously, we identify and then use these patterns to make sense of the world around us. This affects what we decide to believe, resulting in us often being overconfident about our reasoning in a given context—even if we actually know little about the issue. This is obviously often the case when dealing with the complexity of society, ecosystems, and the planet and how we interact—or not—with these. Secondly, we are also influenced by others, including institutions such as media—mainstream or social. Thus, we run the risk of responding in a very automatic way to cues, issues, and information, rather than reflecting on what we are exposed to. And I haven't even made note of the consequences that come from the advent of "fake news."

Instead, critical thinking is such a significant skill to have because, if done well, it has notable flow-on effects to other skills and traits that leaders now require. This includes, but is not limited to, understanding our own assumptions, our blind spots, and a key means by which to move toward leading in response to the storm, namely, an understanding of the "other," be it key stakeholders, communities, or even the natural environment and all this entails. If we have a better understanding, as leaders, of these facets of ourselves, then we can be better informed and make better decisions. In a networked world, experiencing momentous and sometimes hostile change, if we don't make the shift, change will be imposed upon us.

Before I continue, it is worthwhile clarifying what critical thinking entails, as opposed to strategic thinking (namely, the interconnectivity of systems and the parts within). I like Ennis' (1993) thoughts on critical thinking ... "reasonable reflective thinking that is focused on deciding *what* to believe or do." Such thinkers have a disposition to engage in exploration and reflection during this reasoning process; they can search, understand, and *evaluate* information logically and rationally during problem solving and/or decision making (Butler 2012; Shaw et al. 2020). For leaders who have been brilliant at solving linear-style problems, it can be challenging to then consider whether your information sources are appropriate.

We need to almost problematize our sources of information and considerations; just what are we missing? Have we obtained a breadth and indeed, a depth of information to effectively understand what we face? Why are we thinking in a particular way toward the issue?

To be able to decide what to believe or do, Ennis (1993) observes that an individual needs to consider a number of things, interdependently. These include, but are not limited to:

- Being open minded
- Being well-informed
- Finding reasons and assumptions
- Judging the credibility of sources
- Crucially, draw conclusions when called for, but with caution

I really like the powerful simplicity of that as well as the final disclaimer: "with caution." Within your own business do you see leaders who are good at that? Really good at thinking critically. Futures thinking, which I will come to in Chapter 7, can play a significant role in facilitating the above.

Perhaps, that ability to think critically and question our assumptions is also about emotional intelligence—having an awareness of how the behavior of others affects you and alternatively, how your behavior affects others. This is so important as we must be mindful that our cultures and our worldviews can blind us to how we interpret what lies before us (Berglund 2020). This trait doesn't come naturally to many but is just so vital to leaders who want to do something meaningful. This is something I will talk to you about in detail in the next chapter.

Leaders certainly can enhance each of the skills described in this chapter, on their own, and thus facilitate enhanced decision making. However, as seismic shifts in enhancing lives, livelihoods, and the planet are increasingly demanded by stakeholders, Eva has highlighted that the risk of making decisions on your own without considering other perspectives is just too great. As I'll discuss in the next chapter with the further assistance of Gidon, Yana, and Nada from EcoPeace ME, the deployment of these skills reaches its full potential when you approach sustainability or regenerative issues using a collaborative or co-created approach with the key stakeholders that have common interests, diverse perspectives, and expertise.

Before we hear from them, I believe that there is no way that I could build the case for collaboration and co-creation as eloquently or passionately as Eva, who lives this every day and has done so for many years. "The mindset that you and I have been taught throughout our lives and how we and nature have evolved has also always been about competition— that we evolved together by competing with each other. Yet, it's not really true. Humanity would never have come to where we are today with all that magnificent innovation if we hadn't been collaborating. Then we've moved into a competitive mode, and kind of lost track of the importance of collaboration. For us (Houdini), it's been essential really and I want to spread that message because with the challenges we're facing today, of course, it's even more important than ever to collaborate. And it's such a much more beautiful way of evolving, I think, so much more rewarding. I want to get everybody out of that silo. And realize there's so many more opportunities to collaborate. And in our near context, there are sustainable outdoor brands asking for exclusivity for a few seasons before they share it with others. I understand the logic behind it because there's been a lot of investments in it, and so forth but if you really care about sustainability and want to change the world in the right direction, it doesn't make sense to keep it for yourself. It's joyful sometimes to make it very clear that we are open source and share. We've always done it because we have had lots of knowledge in a very certain area, and we've been happy to share that with others. And then we gained so much from it because we get knowledge from others, which we need."

This isn't idle bragging. As a consequence of their collaborative efforts, Houdini and its partners have developed a far more sustainable fabric to the alternative—one that is made from recycled materials and can be broken back down into recycled materials. Yet, contrary to the rest of the industry, Houdini does not intend to place a patent over their intellectual property; rather, the company has a vision of making the industry more sustainable with competitors following this lead as a result of Houdini's openness (Holtström et al. 2019).

"What I think is important is to get out of the degenerative ways and help each other realize that there's such opportunity. And there's so much value we can create if we start thinking in a new way toward regenerative; we must collaborate and we must realize that we're part of the living system. And it's extremely urgent. It's going too slow for me. Yet, I think I'm hopeful as well. I think what we're doing together with others—not alone—is creating great initiatives. We have to start gaining momentum and telling those stories."

Reflections

How does your organization ensure that the "nestedness" that Hahn and Tampe referred to is incorporated into strategic—or event tactical—decision making?

What role could influencers play in your organization with respect to enhancing lives, livelihoods, and the planet?

What assumptions are you bringing to thinking and decision making, conscious, or otherwise? What lessons have you taken away from the impact these have had on resulting decisions and outcomes?

What sources of information do you call on to help with understanding your context?

What means do you call on to unearth individual or organizational blind spots?

– CHAPTER 6 –

ENDING THE RAINS

Individually, we are one drop. Together, we are an ocean.

Ryūnosuke Akutagawa

Ending the Rains

We simply cannot resolve our wicked challenges on our own. As leaders, we simply do not have all the expertise, time, perspectives, or all the understanding required in order to successfully develop a strategy. And even if we did, considering that we are living in an era of increasing outrage where trust in our institutions is in decline, it doesn't make sense to continue foisting direction on stakeholders when it comes to confronting the social, economic, and environmental storm that we face (Figure 6.1).

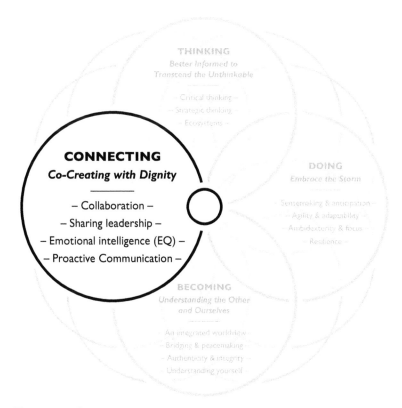

Figure 6.1 Connecting

Co-Creating With Dignity

There are significant benefits for leaders who have a deep desire to advance strategies and solutions by working with those who have a prominent and relevant interest—and indeed, influence. As we've been hearing from the leaders that I've introduced to you, thus far, how collaboration and co-creation are becoming a real necessity because of the strategic benefits that can be created for an organization, namely:

- Improved reputation or brand
- Innovation stemming from a "collision" of ideas and perspectives
- Enhanced market opportunities
- Improved risk management from overcoming the blind spots or constructs inherent in a leader's worldview or mindset
- Engaged staff and stakeholders

Collaboration is viewed by the UN as being so critical to the implementation of the sustainable development goals (SDGs) that were discussed earlier in the book that it has its own goal: SDG 17—partnerships for the goals. All of the goals will require the involvement of, and significant collaboration across, all sectors if we are to accelerate solutions to the different facets of the storm (Stibbe and Prescott 2020).

Nevertheless, old ways of thinking can still restrict us. I have observed many times where organizational leaders think that they are collaborating when, in reality, they are often unconsciously wanting others to simply do what the leader wants them to do. While I want to highlight that leaders should confront that impulse, I will talk about sharing versus controlling leadership a little later on. It's a vitally important consideration to reflect on.

Quite possibly one of the most inspiring organizations that I've ever come across is EcoPeace ME, who I introduced you to earlier. And quite possibly three of the most inspiring and caring leaders that I've ever met are its co-directors Gidon, Yana, and Nada. You may recall me describing the challenges that they face promoting collaboration and restoring hope in a region where there can be so much polarization, so much hatred.

Much of their collaborative efforts focus on the Jordan River Basin, a major source of freshwater in an increasingly water scarce region and an extremely sensitive ecosystem. Upstream, its waters have been over-used due to almost six decades of growing population and increased agricultural and industrial activity, reducing downstream flows to the extent that by the height of each year's summer, the river has virtually dried up by the time it reaches the Dead Sea. Considering that any country that has a supply less than the UN-designated water poverty line of 1,000 cubic meters (m^3) per person per year is deemed to be resource poor with respect to water, and the three countries that are the focus of EcoPeace's work fall into this category (El-Anis and Smith 2013). However, such challenges will only deepen.

The areas of the Upper Jordan River Basin, for example, could see "mean annual temperature increases up to 4.5°C and 25 percent decreases in mean annual precipitation" by the end of the 21st century. When considering this as well as the reasons for overuse described above, countries in the Middle East and North Africa Region are expected to deepen their way into absolute water scarcity (less than 500 m^3 per person per year) by 2050 (Greenwood 2014; Baggio, Qadir, and Smakhtin 2021).

The uncertainty can certainly create tensions as it affects existing power balances—as must be the case between Israel, Palestine, and Jordan. However, it can also strengthen cooperation (Fischhendler and Katz 2013). Thus, their work uses both a top-down, advocacy strategy complemented with a bottom-up, grassroots approach, always collaborating. They are supported by hundreds of volunteers to work on projects that include "Good Water Neighbors," an amazing scheme to raise awareness of the shared water problems that cross-border communities across Jordan, Israel, and Palestine face. In the case of that project, it enhances transboundary cooperation around water availability and sanitation; youth education; and advocating for holistic solutions for the water-energy nexus (EcoPeace 2020).

In that context of leading in the Middle East, I wonder how many people can be truly successful. I suspect that the figures are frustratingly slim. Yet, Gidon, Yana, and Nada are.

It is important to emphasize that collaborations need to be meaningful and respectful toward other parties. Leaders must treat stakeholders with dignity, paying due respect to the standing and worth of stakeholders—and their perspectives—if they are to build trust and extract the best commitment, insights, and ideas. Make no mistake, it's good for business.

Listening to the three of them, it's inspiring to see how readily collaborating with dignity comes to them. It is not a token effort to them or a tick-a-box exercise. Rather, they appreciate that the only chance they have to succeed at improving the "health" of the natural environment and enhancing peace is to be open to the innovation that potentially only results from working with diverse and knowledgeable stakeholders and letting go of control.

As I've already touched upon collaboration in some of the preceding chapters, I'm not going to talk too much about the collaboration process, per se. Besides there are already great writings on *how* to collaborate (Kania and Kramer 2011; and Morrison, Hutchesons, Nilsen, Fadden, and Franklin 2019 spring to mind). Instead, I'll talk more about the key skills and behaviors that underpin good collaboration. However, when it comes to interacting with stakeholders, there are several words that are overused or misused—words like collaboration. So, just what does collaboration mean?

One of the best definitions that I've come across is that from Morrison et al. (2019) who observe that it "involves *linking, leveraging and aligning* resources in ways that enhance one another's capacity to create a shared outcome, a mutual benefit." Key for me within this definition is the creation of shared, beneficial outcomes. To achieve this, the process, the leadership required must also be shared.

Sharing Is Caring

Leadership theories have noted a shift from top-down, bureaucratic models designed for institutionalized hierarchies to often shared or collaborative views of leadership in the age of uncertainty (Kukenberger and D'Innocenzo 2020).

While it is accepted that someone will always be held responsible for achieving particular strategic objectives, there are often occasions now where the best way forward is to share leadership—even when they may be external stakeholders.

Formal leaders often cannot have all the necessary skills or abilities—and time—to effectively lead in a fast-changing, complex environment. And the flow-on effects include an inability to generate creative ideas or solutions and thereby, an inability to adapt to the changing environment (He, Hao, Huang, Long, Hiller, and Li 2020). Enhanced performance and improved decision making, consequently, can result from improving diversity of members and the resulting collision of diverse perspectives and positive tension that generates influence, learning among the group and new knowledge to resolve the challenges faced (He et al. 2020). Now that doesn't mean enhancing diversity for diversity's sake; in the case of the wicked opportunities that organizations have at their disposal, that diversity may come from diversity of appropriate key stakeholder groups involved, expertise and perspectives.

Let's just pause and absorb that; this may require you to also talk with those whom you dislike talking to. How often do you hold those discussions? Make no mistake; you may need to do this because these discussions, as uncomfortable as they may be, are often those where you can learn the most—if you are open to listening *deeply* and respectfully.

I'm sure you have all too often heard about the benefits of calling on diversity in thinking. However, in society, we have deep structural constraints that define who in government/big business/capital cities are to be involved in deciding upon the way forward with respect to our most complex challenges. But this can come with risks that need focused management.

We need diverse ways that remove hierarchical and potentially, blin-kered decision making. We need greater understanding, gained from involving stakeholders with vested interests in these challenges or oppor-tunities related to lives, livelihoods, and the planet.

Leadership may need to be spread across the group. (This doesn't mean that no one has sole responsibilities.) Gidon put it bluntly, reflect-ing on what leadership styles work in the Middle East. "You can't do anything alone, particularly in our context. There's no way that I can understand and be effective in Palestine or Jordan. It's not my culture." This makes so much sense in such a tense, complex, and polarizing sit-uation. Nevertheless, I was struck by something else he noted which I believe is of relevance to many contexts, like your own. "My team have a high level of involvement so that they can come up with their own ideas. For them, there is a real sense of their own investment, resulting."

He alluded to the word "investment" a couple of times. That investment in staff, even stakeholders, their leadership, and what they can provide appears to be so important in providing the confidence necessary to deal with such significantly complex and polarizing situations. The strategic benefits are obvious to Gidon. "When I think of some of our most exciting programs like the Good Water Neighbor, which we've been running for 15 years, it was one of our staff that came up with that idea. He wanted to try it in his community. It worked so well that it was tried in other communities and is led by staff."

No one party seeks to maintain a hold on decision making. Instead, they focus on how, collectively, they can achieve the organization's vision and strategy.

Yana added to Gidon's insights, observing that the leaders invest time in their teams, their understanding, and leadership so that they're "not only empowered, but are *courageous* to make decisions. We'll do it together. And we let small mistakes happen because I know that's the way they will learn."

Going Against the Grain

I cannot imagine how that notion of shared leadership may leave some feeling cynical, suspicious, ambivalent, or even, anxious. We've had leaders successfully overseeing institutional hierarchies for centuries, so why change?

Sharing may not come easy to some. When leaders fear they may lose power and the ability to shape their surroundings at will, there may be harmful consequences. Namely, leaders may prioritize their self-interests over that of staff and exhibit this as bad behavior (Wisse, Rus, Keller, and Sleebos 2019). There is also a very natural fear that leaders may consequently feel that they no longer matter or "be seen" as not creating any value to begin with, that is, imposter syndrome.

When you reflect on it, however, does the "one, true leader" approach make commercial or strategic sense? Or is it just reflective of an ages old story that hasn't adapted? If you dig a little deeper, we can again appreciate how powerful the story of leadership has been when it comes to organizing people. It is also damming.

The story of the "great leader" helps to reinforce the necessity of hierarchies. It is treated as "fact." In times of uncertainty, people take heed of the negative emotions experienced—stress, worry, anxiety, and helplessness—and project them onto "leaders." They attribute belief that leaders will be in control of issues and the underlying chaos, complexity, or what may feel overwhelming. Yet, it is an illusion, a construct (Gemmil and Oakley 1992). How many leaders have "solved" climate change? Poverty, hunger, or any of the other components of the storm that I have spoken about to this point?

Certainly, there will still be a need for someone like you to engage, inspire, and coordinate people and other resources when it comes to strategy or operations. Nevertheless, in the age of uncertainty, you just won't have the time or holistic perspective to make the appropriate decisions and implement them quickly and effectively. We need to democratize leadership, changing the story to a "Team of 5M—or 5Bn—leaders' narrative" (Ross et al. 2021).

But just to reiterate, that doesn't mean that your role is reduced. Your role as a leader, supporting others, has never been more important.

I would like to step in here to clarify this discussion. I am not suggesting that this form of leadership is about being altruistic or subsuming your own views/needs for the good of others. The most effective collaborative leaders are good at expressing the needs of their own organization clearly and succinctly, and good at listening (Archer and Cameron 2012).

"Soft Skills" Provide Such Strength

So why do I think that the three co-directors of EcoPeace were meant to be collaborating on some of the toughest issues in the toughest context imaginable? Well, for each of them, they certainly have the critical and strategic thinking necessary to deal with wicked problems to make improvements to regenerating lives, livelihoods, and the planet. Yet, I also see in each of them a level of emotional intelligence, which is extraordinarily high *and* extraordinarily rare—and an intense sense of purpose, for that matter. I was struck by comments like those from Nada that she wants "to leave this world with something that makes me satisfied, that basically makes me feel that I've done something meaningful."

Just try to imagine the situation that they are in. As Gidon observed, for outsiders this working environment that they are immersed in would appear to be such a hopeless situation. "We work in one of the most challenging regions where, from an outsider's perspective, they would generally say, 'Well, what chance is there to do anything? It's such a hopeless situation we live in, our countries are so hopeless. Our leadership is so hopeless.'"

These three leaders are completely invested in achieving positive outcomes. They are invested in regenerating hope. This requires, as Nada observed, "*a lot* of planning, advocacy, and discussion." They must think very tactically and critically to deliver their programs effectively and keep excellent working relationships with their diverse, polarized stakeholders from across the region. They always must be mindful of how their behavior may affect another. The consequences, otherwise, could be critical. Considering how successful they are leading within the Middle East, it doesn't surprise me just how emotionally intelligent Gidon, Yana, and Nada are.

Tuning in to the Other and Ourselves

What is emotional intelligence in the context of this book? Well, I like this definition, namely, that emotional intelligence is the ability to:

> *tune in to the world, read situations and to connect with others while taking charge of your own life*
>
> —Schein 2009

It really resonates with me. Certainly, it highlights the importance of being mindful of the inner being—that we need to be aware of ourselves in order to live the fulfilling lives that we want. Yet, it pushes us all to fully embrace, and be truly attentive and caring to what occurs around us and to others—including the environment, rather than being consumed by ourselves. Finally, the ability to "read situations" means that a leader needs to look at more than what is happening at the surface. They need to be cognitive of the emotion in others.

Suffice it to say that, when there is going to be a prominent level of interaction anticipated between an organization and influential stakeholders on issues that could get messy, then emotional intelligence will be critical. Sure, emotional intelligence is a term that I am certain you've heard bandied about often over the last 10 years or so. Yet, for all of the talk about it, I'm sorry but why are there still so many who do not exhibit it?

Now, I want to go deeper and introduce Goleman et al.'s (2002) observation about the four traits that make up emotional intelligence, namely:

- *Recognition of one's emotions*: Being conscious and aware of how you are feeling at a given moment, such as angry or stressed.
- *Recognition of emotions in others*: Having the social awareness to see or predict how another individual, group, or organization may be feeling in response to yourself or alternatively, to something else that you may not be aware of.
- *Regulation of emotions in oneself*: When you are angry or stressed, having the ability to control those emotions so that others aren't adversely impacted by them.
- *Regulation of emotions in others*: When there may be a crisis associated with a key stakeholder, the emotionally intelligent leader is able to manage those relationships by recognizing their emotions, regulating these, and being aware of others' emotions.

You know, I get frustrated with emotional intelligence being referred to as a "soft skill." With that, can come an inferred mindset downplaying its importance. From my experience, I cannot emphasize enough how emotional intelligence plays such a critical role for leaders. I believe that it can help facilitate leaders:

- Seeing the ecosystem that lies around them, thereby predicting where issues or risks may exist and synthesizing superficially disparate information into a greater whole to improve decision making.

- When it comes to critical thinking and questioning, the information you receive and your own assumptions in relation to that information.
- Sensemaking in any given situation (which will be discussed in detail in Chapter 7).
- Transitioning to a less mechanistic worldview, respecting the connection between institutions, stakeholders, the wider society, and the natural environment.

Universities and business schools are, increasingly, seeing it as critical to integrate into their curriculum. It has significant worth because those students who can put it into practice will have the enhanced potential to positively contribute to lives, livelihoods, and the planet. Simply put, high emotional intelligence helps leaders to generate cooperation, optimism, and enthusiasm among stakeholders (George 2000). The benefits aren't that "soft," are they?

Enhancing the Chance to Thrive

I completely appreciate that collaborating with government departments or agencies, private companies, such as competitors and suppliers, or not-for-profits is not always easy at the best of times. Egos may need to be managed as well as differences of views and values. I see it repeatedly, where emotions can feel as infectious as the outbreak of any virus, readily influencing others within a group or organization, possibly in a profoundly negative way. Emotions can become disruptive within a work environment (Goleman et al. 2002). This is a challenge as emotions and distrust in a leader can make or break a group effort.

Emotional intelligence, therefore, critically underpins collaborative efforts to find a way to regenerate lives, livelihoods, and the planet. It helps to minimize conflict or gain the most out of conflicts, as well as get the most out of strategic relationships.

It was fascinating as Gidon, Yana, and Nada built a picture of the behaviors associated with emotional intelligence that they believed were vital for collaborative efforts. Humility came up several times. Indeed, one of the key points that came out of the dialogue for me was how emphatic these three leaders were in their shared belief that you just can't achieve anything of substance, alone, in these situations. With humility, as whole heartedly agreed to by the three of them, comes a deep desire for listening—and listening deeply—and to genuinely hear and understand, irrespective of vastly diverse cultures or context.

As an aside, Daniel, Eva, and Zainab also emphasized the importance of humility. "I always say nobody has a monopoly over knowledge," observed Zainab. "When you're a leader, the first thing that you require is to know what are your limitations? What other skill sets do I need to bring to complement my own so that we can address the problem we have before us?" Each of them was emphatically humble, facilitating dignity for the other.

Again, I want to "pause" the conversation briefly to let their critical insights really sink in. Leaders can often subconsciously want to *lead* such conversations to control the direction. There may be a fear there, unwittingly, that things won't go well without your direct intervention. Repeatedly, however, the opposite happens. Such conversations break down or conflict can go underground as people feel like they have not been involved. Listening with humility always brings about benefits.

The EcoPeace co-directors see that they are constantly developing as leaders from gaining a greater sense of awareness about themselves and others. Now, that's humility and curiosity, which play a key role in nourishing the style of leadership that I have alluded to where the leader's purpose is to *serve* the other, whether that be internal or external stakeholders, society, or the planet.

Empathy and compassion toward, and understanding of, the other are also critical. Gidon observed that the historical story across the region is that "we are surrounded by hate. The *other* is the enemy." Mull over that observation and compare the consequences of the critical decisions that you make with their experience. Just how can you sincerely and authentically work *together* to get things done when othering is so close to the surface? Surely our "blind spots" or our unconscious efforts to look for wrongs in the other to justify our own beliefs—or biases—remain strong? Yana so compassionately pointed out that "before I blame the other, just what might I be doing wrong?" That takes a lot of self-awareness! There is a need not only to understand the other's reality but also to understand ourselves because even though these leaders are passionate about facilitating positive outcomes for the region, they readily admit that their tolerance can be tested. "We need to step back a little, take a breath and understand that these complexities will always be there," noted Nada. "Things require a lot of time, which potentially, we will not see that change maybe in our lifetime. That requires a lot of patience and an understanding that whatever we're doing, we need to take small steps until we see a change."

This comment about not seeing real change potentially in her life really touched me.

Yana chimed in on the importance of compassion. "We are working in a context that is contrary to the current mainstream and therefore, to work things out together for the benefit of others in the region, we have to understand each other's context and challenges. For each country, there's a different context where things need to be done in a different way in order to reach the same goals. That requires a lot of thoughtfulness. It makes us more compassionate because we need to support each other in different ways where we need it." This impressed me as wouldn't it be only natural for self-interest and othering to come to the surface?

Gidon, Yana, and Nada readily conceded that things were never easy in their roles. Doesn't that sound like such an understatement? It really requires such a keen sense of self-awareness as it would be extremely easy for a Jordanian, an Israeli, or a Palestinian to see the other as anything but human. Too often stakeholders could be viewed as knowing less than "us," having insights that could be undervalued and indeed, for them to be of less worth. Based on the historical story that surrounds leaders, this is quite common and patriarchal worldview.

Walking in Another's Shoes

There is so much more that I could write with respect to emotional intelligence and the traits within. For the sake of brevity, I've had to make some tough decisions about what I cover here—and what have been covered brilliantly, elsewhere. There are so many terrific books and articles on emotional intelligence. So, I want to highlight just one more of these traits: empathy, as I believe it plays such a huge part in removing othering (which I will discuss in Chapter 8), enhancing understanding, and making a leap toward regenerating lives, livelihoods, and the planet.

Empathy is different to sympathy. While sympathy is that strong feeling to help someone in need, empathy is the ability to understand why a person has a need to begin with (Duff 2017). It is appreciated that, in the past, some have seen empathy as being detrimental to good leadership, that it can set back decision making because of being excessively familiar with, or sensitive to, the needs or views of others. Let's call it out for how it was viewed: it has been seen as a weakness in leaders to have empathy. However, as Holt et al. (2017) observed, "in the increasingly immediate, intimate world driven by rapid change, where there is a call to quickly identify evolving opportunities, the case for empathy in business could not be stronger." Empathy plays such a critical role in providing leaders with good anticipation of the risks that may lie ahead—and where or with whom those risks lie—and good "intel," in general. It is such a powerful trait for leaders to develop as it enables greater value creation for your organization. Remember the value that Diego and David from the Latin American Leadership Academy facilitated in their students even though their students couldn't be pigeonholed as being great students? Diego and David's empathy helped them see something more in the students than the education system could facilitate. Wait until you hear once more from Zainab and her empathy in Chapter 8—immensely powerful.

Holt et al. (2017) argue that it can go so much further than that. Empathy plays an important part in sustaining integrity and reducing the potential for self-inflicted organizational crises. While I was initially surprised by that research, on reflection this makes a lot of sense. Holt et al. (2017) refer to Enron, whose blatant greed and dishonest practices showed a complete lack of regard for the needs of the customers and communities they were meant to serve. A self-centered leader will focus on short-term self-interest, irrespective of the consequences for the "other" and indeed, for the organization. I like the fact that Holt et al. observe that "not only does an empathetic mindset led to greater *service* orientation, but also a serving attitude augments empathetic sentiment." It becomes a powerful self-reinforcing loop as it is linked with developing stronger levels of trust—which leaders are struggling, currently to attain—as well as stronger connections with stakeholders, no matter how dispersed or remote they may be (Duff 2017). This also requires honest and proactive communication skills.

More Than Hitting the Target

Some years ago, I came across the utterly brilliant metaphor of communication as an arrow. Have you ever heard that, before? Imagine you hold a bow and arrow; you draw the bowstring back, and then launch the arrow. Bull's-eye! It has hit the target. That metaphor conveys the way that so many of us communicate and the underpinning assumption, namely, by sending out a groupwide e-mail or a press release or a message in a team meeting without seeking feedback, selectively beforehand or more widely after the event. By communicating the message, we assume that it will hit its target and so what is clear to the leader will be clear to the recipients! Effective expression is assumed to equate with effective communication (Clampitt 2016). Yet is that really the case?

The emotionally intelligent leader realizes that to create and support a collaborative space, they must understand the needs of others, internally or externally. They must be proactive at *two-way* communication. My conversation with Nada, Yana, and Gidon often came back to the importance of strategic, tactical, and *respectful* communication. The EcoPeace leaders actively and engagingly communicate with staff about the organization's vision. Yana nodded, noting "that alone is such a vital skill." Again, it requires empathy—to think about your messaging from the audience's point of view—and storytelling abilities. In many contexts where collaboration is key, the communication of a shared vision is tremendously important. If you don't communicate expectations with influential stakeholders, they will fill the void with their own assumptions.

Yet, for EcoPeace, when it comes to engaging such disparate stakeholders and stirring positive action, a shared vision and its communication could stir up a groundswell of regional hatred. The risks are that significant. Nada emphasized that "the phrasing and the messaging are vital because the way we communicate things is extremely crucial and important in order to basically function within our systems as well. To create a sense of independency between your stakeholders, communication needs to be tailored for each individual country. You need to emphasize the strength of working together and the importance of what each brings. You need to create a narrative that speaks to common interests, of the synergies created and how all parties complement one another—but do so with great care."

This comes back to the key skill of communication and a significant part of communication is the need not only to listen but to listen *deeply*.

Gidon continued with this challenge. "We have to grapple with this horrible reality of hate. We seek to create a narrative that speaks to a common concern and then dissect that in a way that's meaningful to each community so that they can be empowered," he observed. That may mean speaking to water rights in one country, the need to pull ourselves out of poverty in a different country, and water security in another of the three. "We've created a very cohesive narrative that we dance with," he observed.

Now, there's a great word with such relevance: dance. "Dance involves patterns, movement, and creativity" and subsequently, many styles. So too, communications involve the coordination of patterns and meanings, and the orienting of one to the other, interpreting when to talk and when to listen, for example (Clampitt 2016). Thus, two-way communication has inherent numerous styles.

Co-creating strategy with dignity is hugely important when it comes to confronting the storm. Through a collaborative approach, leaders can facilitate intentional, informed, and integrated choices about:

- Where should we be active?
- How will we get there?
- How will we stand out?
- What will be our sequence of moves?
- How will we maximize profits/policy/reputation and minimize costs (Hambrick and Fredrickson 2001)?

Leaders can find "true north" with the affected—those who are more educated, more coordinated, and sophisticated than ever before. However, in the age of uncertainty, the context can often feel fluid, rather than static. Consequently, showing how a leader and an organization will confront the storm is one thing but being able to deliver on that is another. And that's our conversation for the next chapter.

Reflections

Who could you involve in developing more informed strategies? What could that look like?

Would your organization's executive leaders be receptive to collaborating with middle managers? What does that say about the dominant leadership styles?

How do you create the safe space necessary for conversations of such importance?

How do you react in a situation when you do not have the expertise? Are you open to new and innovative ideas and approaches, *particularly when they are not your own*?

What does emotional intelligence look like to you?

How do you feel that your own leadership story informs your understanding of your own behavior or that of other's?

Do you try to view things from another's perspective?

How do you behave toward others when things are not going well, are uncertain, or tense? Why do you believe that many leaders have a need to control situations? Is it borne from here? Or something else?

When you listen to others, do you listen *deeply*?

– **CHAPTER 7** –

THE CLOUDS PART

Life is a series of natural and spontaneous changes. Don't resist them; that only creates sorrow. Let reality be reality. Let things flow naturally forward in whatever way they like.

Lao Tzu

The Clouds Part

Developing a way forward—together—is one thing, requiring a particular set of skills and traits. Yet, *delivering* a way forward is, broadly, a different story. However, don't think of the previous chapter and this one as being physically separate; instead, think of the material as overlapping and fluid (Figure 7.1).

Too often, it is common for organizations to focus solely on the development of a strategy in relation to "solving" a problem. It is very natural because everyone enjoys that opportunity to get creative and to explore. Possibly even the introverts.

Figure 7.1 Doing

It is often a different story when it comes to delivering a strategy. Have you ever had the situation where an organization launches its new strategy or plan with great fanfare … only for the content of the plan to be forgotten when business-as-usual diverts the attention of leaders and staff away from delivering that which is important but not urgent? Have any extreme events like the pandemic had that kind of effect on your organization's plan delivery? The image of the organization as firefighters reflects what happens time and time again.

Doing: Lean Into the Storm

When it comes to regenerating lives, livelihoods, and the planet, delivery—getting things done—is a challenge. It seems to be harder with these big issues due to the speed with which change is occurring, but also because of the diversity of views and concerns of the affected. They're not called wicked problems for nothing. We are also truly challenged by the "A" in a VUCA world—ambiguity; people have different views on what are the root causes of a problem or an opportunity because they are interpreting data in such diverse ways. And let's be clear about that. Even when people may have access to the same data, they can still take away different meanings. This is one reason we don't solve wicked problems; we *deal* with them. So, we need to talk about a complementary, set of skills and traits.

It's Just Not *That* Simple

The case I made at the start of this book centered on the huge challenges that we face and that some leadership styles are now brittle and indeed, irrelevant, in the face of those challenges. Yet, these challenges exist also in the context of a speed of change that can occur at a frightening rate.

This has huge implications for how strategy or plans are delivered. For example, there are many hierarchical organizational cultures who value control and stability. And they operate according to what is documented in detailed five-year strategic or corporate plans. Where, no matter what change occurs during the life of a five-year plan, leaders are still rigid with respect to delivering the actions within the plan. No adaptions will be made irrespective of what seismic change may be occurring. "We will stand firm," as it were.

As your context is no longer stable or perhaps familiar, so too the rigid five-year strategy is no longer viable. Leaders need to understand what is happening now, anticipate how emerging trends may change "the way we do things around here," and pivot where necessary.

The Forest for the Trees

Aligned with what I discussed earlier about the importance of thinking, strategically and critically, has been the challenge for leaders through time of sifting through an array of available information to obtain clarity of their context. Obviously, this has never been easy with leaders being time constrained. So, without clarity, how can appropriate visions, strategy, or actions be implemented with any confidence?

This process of leaders interacting with the circumstances that their organization finds itself in to translate the context faced into *new* meaning and consequential action and organization was coined sensemaking a few decades ago (Weick, Sutcliffe, and Obstfeld 2005). Significant efforts are exerted to make sense when the current state of the environment within which an organization operates is perceived to be identifiably different from what is ordinarily expected in that context.

Three key questions are considered during sensemaking, namely, "what's the story?" "what does it mean?" and "now what should I do?" Through asking these questions, not only does meaning about the context come into existence but, by conveying this meaning to stakeholders, action is enabled. Weick et al. (2005) go on to observe that since sensemaking is not about getting to the truth or getting it right, people can still implement effective actions by simply making sense of the circumstances that they find themselves in.

Yet in an age of uncertainty, there are complications faced with achieving good sensemaking. The concept of VUCA conveys a world that is fast-paced, difficult to predict, and as was experienced during the pandemic, overwhelming. Nevertheless, sensemaking relies on a vast number of cues. Potentially, this requires much time and effort as the sense of leaders needs to be updated as a wicked situation evolves, while information remains fragmented (Christianson and Barton 2021). It also presents difficulties for leaders because sensemaking is retrospective; it is relying on the past.

Issues do not present themselves isolated from what else is occurring in your ecosystem or beyond. They are interconnected. Hence, sensemaking is hampered when a leader is facing strategic issues on multiple fronts. In other words, as the pandemic was occurring, leaders wittingly or unwittingly were facing as O'Driscoll and Bleak (2013) observed, "a whole constellation of crises" that impact on one another including climate change, the economic crisis, and issues around #BlackLivesMatter and #MeToo. Making sense can be extremely difficult in such a context.

The brilliant sensemaking traditionally achieved by the heroic or command and control leader when it comes to linear-style issues is hampered as we experience such turbulent and monumental change. There is constant interruption as we grapple to understand what we face (O'Driscoll and Bleak 2013).

There could be huge value in exploring the approaches that other cultures take to sensemaking and thinking. I'm thrilled to bring fascinating Dr. Jinfeng Zhou into the conversation. Dr. Zhou is the Secretary-General for the China Biodiversity Conservation and Green Development Foundation (CBCGDF). Having started in the mid-1980s, his organization has grown from a sole focus on the protection of birds to becoming one of China's leading not-for-profits. As its name suggests, CBCGDF is dedicated to not only the protection and reintroduction of plants, animals, and ecological communities but also the management of climate change, heritage protection, environmental education campaigns, conservation efforts across the nation's universities, and environmental litigation. And believe me when I say that I am only just "scratching the surface" when it comes to describing the sheer scale of this organization's efforts. For a not-for-profit with 50 staff, this may appear to be an enormous workload across a country as large as China. Yet, they are successful because of the staggering support received from tens of thousands of volunteers and hundreds of grassroot NGOs (cbcgdf.org)!

There must be times when it feels like an uphill battle for both Dr. Zhou and his staff, working courageously to conserve the diversity of our plant and animal species. We are presently in a period identified as being our sixth wave of mass extinctions. Since 1500 AD, the rate of extinction of animals and plants has accelerated due to the impact of humans. However, the rates of extinction for birds, mammals, and amphibians are like those of the five global mass-extinction waves of the past 500 million years. Those probably resulted from meteorite impacts, massive volcanism, and other cataclysmic forces rather than us (Tilman, Clark, Williams, Kimmel, Polasky, and Packer 2017).

The causes of the current waves are varied, including habitat destruction, land use change, invasive species, chemical pollution, overpopulation, and overexploitation through fishing and hunting. Such impacts already threaten 25 percent of all *remaining* mammal species, 13 percent of all bird species as well as over 21,000 other species of plants and other animals, with extinction (Pievani 2014; Tilman et al. 2017). It is a massive crisis.

A Team of 10,000

I am anticipating that a linear way of thinking would positively leave Dr. Zhou unimpressed in his sensemaking efforts. He does not rely solely on his own senses and intellect to undertake the situation(s) that he finds himself in; instead, he maximizes his effectiveness by trusting the people he has at his disposal—his staff and the enormous number of volunteers.

"We have many teachers, and we learn first from the people. In China, there are many people that have innovative ideas, new creative ways, who are working on environmental matters, currently. They come to us— they want to do this; they want to do that. We learn from these people about what is happening because we are open to these people. But, we also learn, internationally." For a man of his own international prominence, Dr. Zhou is truly humble about how CDCGDF learns from other nations. "There are so many great practices. So, firstly, we learn and secondly, we try to practice skills on a small scale before we expand." The sensemaking takes place with the involvement of stakeholders in several prominent, highly visible ways. "We publish our learnings and then we receive comments and criticism. We make changes, consequently, and we are very open to responses—many are not good! But we keep on working, we keep on running, learning to improve our service."

Now, one particularly difficult challenge of leading in the age of uncertainty is the amount of information now available. In terms of the data available, I came across an article which said that the "total amount of data created, captured, copied, and consumed in the world is forecast to increase rapidly, reaching 59 zettabytes in 2020" (Holst 2021). I didn't know what a zettabyte was, either! Just two zettabytes of data were consumed in 2010 but this is forecast to jump to 149 zettabytes by 2024. That's a huge increase. (I've just done a quick search and seen that a zettabyte is the equivalent of 10^{21} bytes.) That is a massive number that, if like me, you're finding hard to get your head around. The reason I have shared this with you is to convey just how much data are "out there" and hence, how leaders are subjected to a potential information overload. How can you cut through copious amounts of information to understand the story and what you should be doing?

Indeed, the challenge with the speed of change faced is that it is impossible to predict what will happen next, worsened by decisions often being made without having enough information at hand—or for some, too much information. Knowledge of how one goes about understanding the unfamiliar is therefore more valuable and practical than trying to absorb what might be known today in a technical sense (O'Driscoll and Bleak 2013).

Anticipating the Future, Understanding the Past and Present

It is not only the here and now that aids leaders when it comes to sensemaking. They need to be anticipatory. If we have a sense of what may lie ahead of us, then we can be better informed and better prepared. But that doesn't come naturally to us; even as the future disrupts, we are still tied to old patterns of behavior (Inayatullah 2008). So, for me anticipation (futures thinking or foresight) is one of *the* critical skills now required.

Years ago, I realized that I was failing the communities and organizations that I served from time to time when it came to assisting them in relation to strategic planning for the social, economic, and environmental issues that they face. Have a think about the breadth of such issues that are felt in the community that you live in. There are a lot, right?

When it came time to facilitate conversations with real depth on what did these communities see as *the* critical issues emerging or even what may strategically lie ahead of them in coming years, the conversation just never left the present. Or the past, for that matter. My theory was that people came to these meetings armed with sensemaking that was often based on what cues they had received in the present—or sometimes stories about the glorious past. I struggled to engage them in conversations about the implications of emerging issues at a local, national, or international level. Instead, we discussed broken footpaths or a local government building not being open after 4:30 p.m. on a Friday to pay bills. Not exactly the most prominent issues faced!

Similarly, it is difficult for leaders to develop or deliver their visions and strategy if they are unable to anticipate—but not predict—what future(s) may lie ahead of them—bumps, shocks, crises, and opportunities. We are entering uncharted territory where the past is no longer a workable predictor of the future. Yet, the situation for leaders is worsened by leaders struggling to free themselves from old habits and styles and stories. It is difficult to fully grasp what options for the future may lie ahead. Anticipatory or futures thinking enables leaders to get a glimpse into different options for the future. What do scenarios of the future look like? How do they "feel" (Ross et al. 2021)?

Through being better informed, we can make better decisions. Oh, by the way, did you see how I just referred to "future(s)?" There isn't just one future forming just beyond our fingertips. Rather, there are possible, plausible, and preferable futures before us. The preferred future for you, as a leader, and your organization is based on the actions taken starting in the here and now.

There is significant value in creating different images of what the future may look like, which is most likely to occur, and the insights gained from determining what a future preferred by an organization looks like (van der Laan 2008). Do you remember what Zainab had observed about Africa's experience resulting from the pandemic and the lessons learned? She had reflected that there were issues that numerous African governments had not appreciated to be critically important should moment change take place. This has exacerbated weaknesses or vulnerabilities in the socioeconomic system. Yet, I am sure this isn't just isolated to Africa. The age of uncertainty has highlighted just how brittle our long-standing systems are and we had not anticipated that. A key point that I want to make here is that, in a time when literally anything can happen, it is dangerous to rely solely on what we know today—our stories and accompanying assumptions. The use of futures thinking or strategic foresight will be vital to anticipate what are the next seismic waves we may experience and how we—our leaders, organizations, and systems—can be better prepared.

Importantly, anticipatory or futures thinking enables leaders not only to understand where their organization wishes to head but also to understand the entrenched, historical narratives that the organization unwittingly adheres to. It, therefore, also enables leaders to reflect on their own worldviews, experience epiphanies, and genuinely appreciate how their mindset contributes to the organization's status quo. The narrative is crucial. How do they see themselves? What is the internal story they tell themselves (Ross et al. 2021)? This is crucial for leaders to ensure that the old ways of thinking and doing aren't a hindrance to working toward a preferred future. But, beware that on the path to such a future, in the age of uncertainty, there may still be bumps that we must adapt to.

Agility Not Fragility

Think about the global challenges faced in the last 10 or so years and what that has instigated: the global financial crisis, terrorism, the war in Syria, #MeToo and #BlackLivesMatter, climate change and the loss of biodiversity, and the COVID-19 pandemic. Each of these has tested the robustness of organizations that valued stability and/or ignored the dominant mindset. Many have been found wanting, shown to be brittle.

I referred previously to the ubiquitous strategic plan and how, irrespective of the change that occurs during their life cycle, too many leaders rigidly keep focus on or adherence to the comprehensive content. *No matter* how things change, the plan's content stays solidly unchanged. Unfortunately, in an increasingly VUCA world, we can expect that there will be volatile change, forcing significant impacts if leaders don't adapt.

Informed by sensemaking and anticipation, implementation, particularly when it comes to regenerative practices, requires the capability to respond to changes in the business environment with actions that are focused, fast, and flexible. It requires leaders who are agile and reflective, based on the feedback received from such systems (Horney, Passmore, and O'Shea 2010; Hahn and Tampe 2021). Continuous sensemaking and anticipation are necessary.

Feeling for the Stones

As seen with the pandemic and climate change and can be anticipated with other components of the storm is that successful leaders will be able to anticipate or identify strategic challenges and respond in a prompt or brisk manner. Unlike the leadership styles inherent within institutional hierarchies that are unable to cope with a constant state of flux, the speed of change being seen is a catalyst for leaders to liberate their thinking and organize work in shorter cycles with progress monitored and evaluated at every stage. The agile leader reviews, learns, and adjusts.

Assessment of progress is evaluated more often than would be the case for a traditional strategic plan (Denning 2015). However, this is possible by removing the need for control by the leader and enabling self-organizing teams, networks, or ecosystems to determine how to deliver a vision or strategy. Delivery requires discipline and belief in staff and stakeholders.

From my time with Dr. Zhou, I enjoyed learning about the Chinese saying "cross the river by feeling for the stones" that is universally applicable to an agile mindset. The metaphor of the river implies a swift current and murky waters that can embody the external and internal pressures faced by an organization. It implies unfamiliar territory and uncertainty in how we should proceed; it is too easy to get washed away! Therefore, the agile leader needs to have the right balance between the provision of strategic guidance to staff and stakeholders, thereby reducing chaos, and enabling people to sense and respond to the emerging issues—hence, "feeling for the stones" (Horney et al. 2010). This highlights once again how important communication in the form of a dance is for a leader— how important it is to truly listen and see how the parts are connected. Just as important, this highlights the need for leaders to be flexible and adaptable in how a vision or strategy is met.

Let's hear how CBCGDF has been tactically agile, flexible, and adaptable. "You know, we started in 1985; we were called the China Parrot Diversity Foundation, re-introducing species to China. Later on, we changed our name to China Biodiversity Conservation Foundation. Then after some more years, we saw towards the end of last century that we needed to quickly get serious about development that changed the environment. So, we changed our name again (to CBCGDF). We adapt, we must change," he observed.

> Like we received a call, which resulted in us setting up a new system to establish conservation areas for some species. We did it within one night (!). No one thought that we could do this, but we did. We support the theories of grassroots NGOs across the country. We must be creative and so, can't just stick to strategic plans. This flexibility and adaptation may even require lobbying the government to create legislative change around wildlife protection. Last year, we achieved over 100 laws, regulations and policy changes. And I want to mention the pangolin; in 2020, we had protection of the pangolin upgraded. We also had pangolin scale taken off the China pharmacopeia (that's an official list of medicinal drugs), which was an amazing achievement. We must change. Sometimes we change every day.

I am not suggesting that, tactically, you enable change at the speed that Dr. Zhou has accomplished. Nevertheless, I wanted to share with you how open he is to adapt quickly based on the needs of his tens of thousands of stakeholders. This requires the ability to lead while sharing control and extremely high emotional intelligence on his part.

Ambidexterity

While there is the proliferation of data available to leaders, holistically, there is also polarity in the context faced, reflective of increasing ambiguity in an increasingly networked world. All of this can distract a leader from remaining focused on that which is important. Namely, focusing on the delivery of a vision, strategy, or plan, and increasingly meeting the needs of an array of influential stakeholders.

For the last two decades, you may have heard about the research into the notion of organizational ambidexterity and the benefits that ensue for focus and performance. Rather than having transactional and transformational leadership separated within individual organizational roles, there are benefits in combining these forms of leadership to complement each other (O'Reilly and Tushman 2004; Chebbi, Yahlaoul, Vrontis, and Thrassou 2017).

Sure, this creates a constructive tension that instigates organizational benefits. Perhaps, this still works when confronting linear-style problems. But is it enough when facing the storm in an age of uncertainty? It is worthwhile exploring the Asian view of ambidexterity at the very least since the strategic environment faced by leaders can often be characterized as simultaneously possessing what Zhang, Waldman, Han, and Li (2015) refer to as "two seemingly mutually exclusive assumptions or conditions conflicting demands of inside and external stakeholders." In these situations, I see the individuals who hold disparate views on something as feeling like their perspectives are logical—and indeed, they are. Yet, there can then be a feeling that an individual has a monopoly on the truth because the alternate perspectives or meanings may be polar opposites and therefore, shunned when it comes to further consideration.

The Western mindset of breaking the whole, bigger, picture down into separate, "bite size pieces" that are easy to manage is inadequate for regenerating lives, livelihoods, and the planet when leaders are likely to face contradictory, or seemingly paradoxical, demands (Zhang et al. 2015). Indeed, this is what I see in so many differing situations. Leaders cannot fathom how to deal with, or process, paradoxes. Paradoxes that many struggle with while others already see the interconnectivity, such as short termism versus the long term; agility and adaptability versus focus; shareholders versus stakeholders; self-centeredness versus "other-centeredness."

And important to the book is economic growth versus regeneration.

Instead, operating unquestionably according to the old story, many leaders just revert to the ways that they are comfortable with as they yearn for stability and control.

"Both–And"

So, it is vital to appreciate that the extent to which you and your leaders engage in holistic or integrated thinking is linked to the ability to think ambidextrously. If you are going to be able to deliver long-term success as a leader, then the paradoxes and seeming contradictions must be accepted and indeed, harmonized, thereby creating opportunities to thrive rather than threats to survival (Smith and Lewis 2011).

Leaders must therefore "lean in" to the seemingly chaotic and contradictory situations facing them. They cannot design the difficulties away but need to appreciate that these paradoxes are connected and integrated into a larger order, and by doing so, find opportunities for "dynamic coexistence" (Zhang et al. 2015).

There is much for leaders to learn and reflect on when considering Eastern or Asian worldviews which *naturally* embrace, integrate, and transcend these opposites. Challenges faced aren't viewed as being "either–*or*" the way that Western worldviews analyze and compartmentalize situations. Instead, they are interrelated and viewed as "both–*and*." These seeming opposites coexist harmoniously. Can I ask you to humor me and read that and think about it one more time, please? I believe that is hugely important because in the Yin–Yang philosophy, what may appear to oppose, negate, or separate one from another is connected, complementary, and creating a harmonious whole (Zhang et al. 2015; Li 2016). That is such an important reflection for Western leaders.

Dr. Zhou put it like this:

For leaders, 'Yin and Yang' is both a thought and an active tool. It will help the leader think about problems in a dialectical way, consider and analyze their shared growth in contradictions, and see the opposing sides of everything—the positive in the negative and the negative in the positive. This creates different ideas and different solutions, as a result. The mutual strengths make it possible to adapt to the current situation. Be aggressive while remaining prudent; when you are triumphant, be mindful that you could be easily trapped; in the face of difficulties, we must also actively push forward and persevere.

For leaders who have not considered the bigger picture from this perspective, Dr. Zhou recommended being mindful of it and then taking things step by step, never getting too far ahead of yourself. Dr. Zhou gave the example where a certain percentage of each Chinese Province must be revegetated under national government plans. "It sounds good and requires big planting programs. In one large city, planting trees was to take place in a coastal area. However, we had some volunteers tell us that this was not the right thing to do. They should not be planting trees on the coastal area, because that is an intertidal wetland area, which is feed land for birds and is also the homeland for much marine life. 'They should not be planting trees, there!' And when the matter was raised with the city's authorities, the officials understandably observed that, by planting the correct trees, it would be an important carbon offset and besides, in a city where there was no other land available, the tree planting was part of a great nationwide plan with given targets for carbon offsets." So, what can you do?

Well, Dr. Zhou proceeded to show how Yin and Yang thinking helps to consider the contradictions, together. "The officials worked to find the right trees to plant on the muddy, coastal land. But, how to resolve the conflict? Well, CBCGDF published a critique of the approach on its website and gained much input from its stakeholders. It was pointed out that the wetland was also a carbon offset; it was important, holistically, to appreciate that trees are seen above the land, but it is also important to consider carbon offsets below the land and under the sea. In fact, the natural coastal area is a bigger carbon offset and has so much important marine life that was important to tourism. Therefore, the officials were told that they should see the planting as a 'group program'. The wetlands are good for their program, and while it may not look nice to them, it would offset five times what the tree planting could. It can be complicated, but we try to learn and leverage what we are faced with and minimize the negative and maximize the positive." Holistic ways are always important.

Keeping an Eye on the Bigger Picture

Leaders who can integrate the complexity faced—aided by ecosystems thinking—transcend the heroic leader story. They lead comfortably with the knowledge that their views and insights are but just one perspective. With compassion and humility, they accept divergent perspectives or values rather than see conflicts and seek solutions or ways forward that are holistic in nature and combine divergent views (Tadmor, Hong, Chao, Wiruchnipawan, and Wang 2012).

Certainly, this helps when it comes to gaining access to better, more holistic, information and therefore, better decision making. It is important to be adaptable and to be flexible in delivering on your strategies. Yet, as I had alluded to earlier, it is also important to be clear about just what is important. For me, this is a huge skill. In the age of uncertainty, it is all too easy for organizations, metaphorically, to behave like firefighters, "putting out" all urgent but nonimportant issues while leaving no time or attention for delivery of organizational vision, strategy, or programs. Subsequently, a focus on the whole, but also the bigger picture for your organization, is necessary. Just what is it "we" are trying to achieve? What progress have we made? Has something changed, which we need to adapt to?

Looking After Yourself

Even though I won't talk about this for long, this is an area that I am passionate about.

In the age of uncertainty, resilience is vital. I write this aware that there are leaders who may roll their eyes at that as a cliche. Or a sign of weakness. Yet, dealing with the most wicked of problems is *never* easy, no matter how experienced a leader is. It can force us to confront the embedded leadership story that we adhere to, pushing against a lifetime of habits and shattering beliefs about self, others, and the future (Seligman 2011). It can be draining.

I'm sure that you have a great view of what resilience entails. Sure, it's about "bouncing back" and managing your energy levels when you have too much on your plate; but it's about more than that. It's also about leaders like yourself drawing on your experience to accept the present for what it is and then to positively look to the future (Lawton Smith 2017). As much as you may be influenced by your own leadership story, we simply cannot control as much as we would like. Lawton Smith (2017) also made me reflect on how leaders can lose resilience when they must fundamentally re-evaluate their beliefs because of the issues they face.

I have no doubt that will be the case for many leaders when it comes to authentically confronting the storm.

I have no concern whether you think there is a better term than "resilience" or whether you feel this section is a waste of time. I hope that you are looking after yourself, now and into the future. Just as we need to confront the storm, so too we need to confront ourselves. Confront our story, our values, and worldviews. Are they still relevant as change whirls about us? I say that admitting that I cannot appreciate just what you have on your plate. I don't have to tell you that O'Driscoll and Bleak (2013) observed that leaders experience much loneliness and significant pressure. Leadership can be isolating, right? So, resilience is vital.

As we are nearing the end of "our conversation," we will dig deeper in the coming chapter, exploring our personal, deeper issues of identity and worldviews that underpin our ability to confront the storm. There's going to be much to reflect on about ourselves.

Reflections

What's your organization's story, currently and historically? What does it mean? What should you do now?

Who do you involve when you need to make sense of what the current situation is and what it means? Are you open to widely different views like Dr. Zhou?

What assumptions do you have about the future? What implications does that have for your organization? And how do you manage these assumptions?

Do you feel that you are a leader that "leans into disruption," exploring where there is an opportunity and/or need to adapt? Do you do so in a brisk, even collaborative, manner? What does that look like?

How do you or your team view contradictions? Are the negatives associated with a context ignored and isolated from the focus? What has this meant for the quality of strategies delivered? How could the positives and negatives be better contemplated, holistically?

Are you a firefighter? Or do you have laser-like focus? What does this mean for how you operate in an age of uncertainty?

Do you readily bounce back? What do you do to look after yourself? Do you have a clear sense of purpose?

– **CHAPTER 8** –

HERE COMES THE SUN

We are all visitors to this time, this place. We are just passing through. Our purpose here is to observe, to learn, to grow, to love ... and then we return home.

Australian Aboriginal Proverb

Here Comes the Sun

Do you remember the passionate claims from the leaders that I've introduced you to with respect to the storm placing people, communities, the environment, and organizations at risk? When I interviewed each of them, I often felt the hairs stand up on the back of my neck as I observed this "flow" of concerns conveyed by them. We simply cannot rely on small or incremental enhancements to lives, livelihoods, and the planet. I need to reiterate this point here, one that is key to the argument I am making—that it is in the best interests of leaders to reflect on their style of leadership and confront the need to shift authentically toward a regenerative mindset. In an increasingly networked world, not to mention in an era of outrage, organizations can be left potentially brittle in response to protecting their reputation, brand, profitability, or viability, to name but a few (Figure 8.1).

Becoming: Understanding the Other ... and Ourselves

Therefore, we need to consider the deeper issues such as the way that we see the world and consider ourselves in relation to such "externalities." I know this may have been provocative for many leaders to absorb. I can really connect with Lawton Smith's (2017) observations that a significant challenge for leaders is when they are confronted by issues that *force* them to re-evaluate their beliefs and values; issues like those described in this book. Yet, unlearning and relearning can stimulate the most amazing epiphanies.

We've been considering that new ways of thinking, connecting, and doing are necessary for leaders over the past few chapters. But this just won't happen because of me arguing my thoughts and beliefs with you, no matter how compelling or otherwise I may be in that regard! And I am mindful that this may not happen because of the amazing insights

Figure 8.1 Becoming

provided to you by Zainab, Diego and David, Dr. Grundtland, those three amazing leaders within EcoPeace (Gidon, Yana, and Nada), Daniel, Milena, Eva, or Dr. Zhou. Obviously, *you* must be the one who sees that change is necessary and that the storm is here and has some bearing on your organization. Yet, I hope that I have been able to influence you to let go of some of your thoughts and beliefs along the way and get you thinking about ways to ensure that you won't be lying awake at night contemplating how your organization will overcome future shocks, bumps, and crises.

As part of that, I want to go much deeper and talk to you about your "becoming" rather than being. Bear with me.

The Great Illusion

When discussing humans as a species, the well-known historian Yuval Noah Harari talks about the power of illusions. Our lives, the way that we work, I suppose our worldviews as well; they are all in essence what he portrays as illusions. If you haven't read any of his work, he observes that what really separates *us* as a species from others on the planet is our ability to create stories. Stories that not only have meaning but also compel others in large numbers to commit to cooperating and organizing, providing structure out of chaos (Harari 2011; Forte 2019; Spencer and Monterro Salvatico n.d.).

Stories have been tremendously impactful in the way that they have been utilized to facilitate such cooperation through the years and deliver the progress we have experienced. Yet, as vital as stories are to society, these ordering stories are often nothing but fiction. That's right, the stories that we have complied with for centuries about the great leader are a construct and therefore, create significant obstacles for regenerating lives, livelihoods, and the planet. Stories have implications for the leader and how *they* will view their surrounding environment and how *they* will act or not in relation to that.

The prevalent worldview that we come across in western organizations and societies is reflective of these stories. Such worldviews just aren't successful on their own in shifting us from being subjected to wicked problems to being open to wicked opportunities—from scarcity to abundance. It doesn't acknowledge the limitations of unlimited growth, "the intimate connection between humans and nature and the relationship of the economy to nature" (Kennedy, McGouran, and Kemper 2020).

To be able to deal with what we face requires an appreciation that we and the economy are not separate from "what lies at the front door" of every organization. For leaders wishing to make the giant leap from linear to nonlinear and wicked, this can require a giant leap in the way we see others and the planet—and the value that they provide.

Just as I argued with Dr. Zhou's help that leaders can benefit in the age of uncertainty from taking on ways of doing in line with Asian worldviews, so here I am arguing that leaders need to contemplate ways that they can learn from. Ways they may be able to integrate into their work if they are to ensure that not only do their organizations remain successful and viable, but they as leaders do, too. Obviously, this is not a quick fix. As Li (2016) observed, this is about "becoming," rather than "being."

Being infers a process that is fixed has certainty and a complete form of existence. Becoming, on the other hand, is independent of, and interactive with, others. It's spontaneous and nonlinear, conveying personal growth, compared to "being."

Just as there are real benefits to you as a leader from reflecting on Dr. Zhou's insights and putting those into practice when it comes to "doing," so too, there are benefits to leaders from reflecting on Indigenous worldviews or ways of becoming. Indigenous worldviews take a holistic view of guardianship, caring for the environment and society *to maintain strong economies* (Kennedy et al. 2020). For leaders in western organizations to access the opportunities available, they must remove that compartmentalized way of seeing lives, livelihoods, and the planet as separate to the work undertaken by their institutions as so many do. There is much that we can learn from Indigenous ways to successfully confront the storm.

I have had the opportunity to hold many conversations with Indigenous people. When I ask "what do you love about home?" irrespective of their standing in society, they always blow me away with the eloquence and power of their responses. That was also my experience when listening to the deeply caring Dr. Dalee Sambo Dorough and wise Oren Lyons.

Dr. Dorough is a human rights lawyer and the current Chair of the Inuit Circumpolar Council (ICC), a major international NGO that champions a number of political, cultural, and environmental causes for the 180,000 Inuit people across Alaska, Canada, Greenland, and Chukotka (Russia). Working in forums such as the Arctic Council and the United Nations, the ICC has played an influential role in multilateral discussions around contentious issues such as climate change, persistent organic pollutants, Arctic security, and regional autonomy (ICC 2021). This voice, observed Smith and Wilson (2011), has challenged the state-centric status quo and dominant economic ideologies that shape the world currently, countering Western scientific constructions of the world.

Dr. Dorough told me how her roots are in Northwestern Alaska. As that is a long way from my home city, I asked her about what "home" means for her. Her eyes lit up with joy. "I had this funny conversation with the postman, recently, who happens to be from the same village.

Having a conversation at that time of year is when silver salmon arrive, when blueberries are ripe, and he observed just how much he missed the smell of the place. And I knew right away what he was talking about! Everything!"

Isn't that such a fantastic and vivid way to describe "home?"

As our conversation went deeper, I quickly realized how Dr. Dorough's worldview saw something more sophisticated and holistic than my Western worldview would allow. "It's not only about the connection, but the relationships to everything around you and understanding that you're a species within that environment, like all the other species. You're not the one that has any power or control over it. You're a part of that ecosystem and those *profound* symbiotic relationships, with everything around you, are so important. That sense of identity, wholeness, overall wellness, and belonging is really empowered by those relationships and the care that you give and receive. We've always had this."

Unlike the Western worldviews that I've discussed, Graham (2008) noted that Indigenous thinking and meaning flows from two important kinds of relationship in life. They are (i) those between people and the land and (ii) those among people, themselves (although that is still contingent on land). Therefore, all meaning comes from the land. As Dr. Dorough observed, that meaning comes from the animate *and* inanimate. There is something critical in this way of thinking when it comes to the seismic challenges now faced.

Do you think that those relationships will be important to your organization for the future? If not, then why not? I think that is an important question for leaders to reflect on. *Why not?*

The Storm: An Indigenous Perspective

Having conceded early in the book that I struggled to convey to you the extent of the storm, Dr. Dorough was able to skillfully provide insights on what is being faced in the far north, insights that left me feeling numb and anxious. Remember how I had noted that management academics Bennis and Nanus had witnessed change in the mid-1980s within the work environment for leaders? Well, there was already a lot more going on than that.

"The storm is here. You know, our people attended the UN Conference on Environment and Development in 1992, in Brazil. Even at that time we were seeing changes, and nobody was paying any close attention to that. This is kind of what we've been telling you—that the changes are here and they're dramatic. It's been that way for *decades*."

Inuit people have a profound relationship with their lands and territories with their environmental knowledge accumulating through countless generations. They have needed this knowledge as their ability to be healthy depends upon a healthy environment (Dorough 2021). It's not just climate change that is observable to Inuit. "We're not really talking about a single storm; we're talking about one compounding another, you know. They're layer after layer after layer. Having the ability to express and identify all of them is becoming harder and harder because everything is so interrelated. Even that connection to land, to the coastal seas and oceans—everything is interrelated."

This is concerned, even with what we face from climate change, alone. The most recent work from the Intergovernmental Panel on Climate Change has observed that the impacts and risks are becoming more difficult to manage as multiple climate hazards occur simultaneously. Risks will interact, resulting in compounding overall risk. Ominously, the IPCC observes with high confidence that some responses to climate change will result in new impacts and risks (IPCC 2022). And, like I said, that is just for climate change.

This is placing unbearable stress on northern peoples like the Iñupiat.

Dr. Dorough had described the cultural/spiritual relationship that these people in northern Alaska have, specifically, with the bowhead whale. The Iñupiat people (Iñupiat is the people; Iñupiaq is a person) call themselves the "People of the Whales" with their worldviews having revolved around the whales that they hunt, consume, and revered for 1,000s of years (Sakakibara 2011). Dr. Dorough continued, "There's this extraordinary relationship that they have because they wouldn't exist if it weren't for that relationship. They would never have adapted to be able to harvest such a massive, multi-ton marine mammal."

For the Iñupiat people, the increasingly warming oceanic temperatures influence the migration patterns and timing of the ice-loving bowheads, making it harder for Iñupiaq to hunt the whales. As the sea ice thins and the waters warm, the whales now must take a further northern route to get to their summer feeding ground. However, the distance between their migration path and these Iñupiat communities is increasing (Sakakibara 2011).

We're also world-renowned for wild salmon. This season, the runs have been really poor. The returns are shocking. In fact, maybe this will paint a clearer picture. There was a Yup'ik man who started fishing when he was six years old. He and his father would go out every year and their target was 300 fish that they approximately needed for his extended family that would carry them through the winter. He's now probably 70 years old and he says that the number of fish he has in his freezer right now is one.

Their food system is collapsing.

The first to feel the brunt of it (the storm) are our people because, for this man and to Yup'ik, their keystone cultural species is the salmon. And you know, every year for the last 15 to 20 years, it's a perennial crisis of low returns of salmon. Then you have the commercial fisheries, the sport hunters, and all policies and regulations are not geared towards the people who've depended upon it for centuries. Of all the impacts that are emerging, food security is at the core, especially as we talk about climate change. People are losing their lives because of melting sea ice due to climate change, and their pursuit of walrus who typically climb on to the sea ice for birthing, resting, or for a whole host of things. The changes are dramatic.

Yet because the layers of the storm are interrelated, we know that when even just one part of a system is not working, the entire system is impacted (Begay 2021). "My background is human rights," noted Dr. Dorough. "When I work with young people, I remind them that one of the key elements about human rights is that they are interrelated and indivisible. If you impact or affect one, it's going to have an impact on all of your other rights—your economic, social, cultural, spiritual, and political rights." So, while leaders may wish to break things down into smaller components, they also must think holistically.

So many Indigenous communities, as Dr. Dorough noted, have been seeing the storm for decades. Indeed, it was because I had used the phrase "the storm" in my introductory discussion with her that she was insistent that I talk to 91-year-old Oren Lyons.

He is a Faithkeeper—an appointed caretaker—of the Onondaga people of western New York state or Haudenosaunee territory. Lopez (2007) observed that Oren carries himself with the unaffected manner of elders in many of the world's indigenous traditions—unpretentious, understated. While I "only" got to talk to him over the phone, I could clearly hear the authority in his voice, even from afar.

His wisdom is grounded in a recognition and acceptance of human responsibility where all forms of life are concerned (Lopez 2007). When I mentioned the storm to him, he observed that he had been witnessing it for 50 to 60 years across the "wonderful, powerful, natural world. I've watched lots get deteriorated and I've watched the acceleration. I see two problems facing our humanity today: one, is the compounding effect of the ice melting. And the other, the compounding effect of an increasing human population. Those elements, together, produce an existential crisis. You're dealing with natural forces that are beyond control."

There's that word "control" again. But, back to the compounding effects he was describing. "Going back to 1950, I was 20 years old, and the earth's population was around 2.5 billion people. Now, 70 years later, the population is almost eight. In one lifetime, that is not sustainable. The human population is going to continue to compound, not just compounding." The latest forecasts are for the global population to reach around 10 billion by 2050 with countries in the sub-Saharan Africa region, alone, could account for more than 50 percent of this growth (Baggio et al. 2021).

"That human population demands water. It demands a place to live and then demands subsistence. And as you can see, there are lotteries apparently around the world. Some people have a lot, some people have almost none." As was also implied by Diego and David, Oren didn't believe that there were any serious efforts by world leaders to deal with this.

Secondly, "ice is melting all over the world. Melting fast in the Arctic and Antarctic. It's melting in the mountains. It's melting everywhere. The world is heating up and has been for some time now. There is transformation taking place that's going to affect everybody and everything. It's not waiting for people to understand."

Moving on, Oren's wisdom reminded me of something that Dr. Dorough mentioned: "I was the chair of the UN Permanent Forum on Indigenous Issues when the sustainable development goals were being discussed. And, of course, my first line was *we're* the inventors of sustainable development. We have much to share with you about sustainable development!" Why was I reminded of that? Well, hopefully I have conveyed that Indigenous worldviews take a holistic view of the environment, society, and economies. It is a worldview that is nonhuman centered, almost like what was covered in my description of an ecosystem in Chapter 5. Oren put it like this, "Indigenous people live with nature. Nature is not bound to them; they are in nature. So, you're very much aware of what changes are happening. And the changes are quite extreme and have been for some time."

While the involvement of Dr. Zhou previously was to get you thinking about the need for adaptability and agility, the involvement of Dr. Dorough and Oren was to convey the need to keep the big picture in mind. Indigenous worldviews are strategic and look to the long term. Native Americans, for example, have an awareness to think about the fate of the upcoming generation (Graham 2008; Pukan 2016). Indeed, it was quite poignant when Oren discussed this mindset. "I used to think, even 40 years to 50 years ago, that my great, great grandchildren are going to have a hard life. And I can see that they're going to be fighting for their life because of the lack of water." There were no words that I could call on in response.

There's Always the Next Day

There is a critical message that you can take away from these stories. A key trait for leaders is to understand that no one worldview provides enough diversity in "truth" and understanding for leaders to be able to successfully confront the storm of wicked problems coming their way (Morgan 2020). As I write this, I have a smile on my face in anticipation of the bewilderment that I may be creating for you. "Does he really think *that* is going to happen at my work?!" I'm not suggesting that you *suddenly* must make seismic changes; the examples I have provided in this book were meant to be "small, practical steps" that could be readily implemented. However, through exploring what we face from the different perspectives described, the resulting critical thinking can offer us the opportunity to question, well, what we take for granted in the way we see the world and learn, accordingly. I am arguing that these different worldviews can help us to reflect on how our views may even hinder our ability to strategically deal with the bigger issues and, by doing so, improve the way that we strategically lead.

I argue this, extremely aware that even though conditions are changing, worldviews and values don't readily change (Morgan 2020). Yet, in the "illusion" of the heroic or command and control leaders and their journey, hasn't there always been competing views on issues? No one leader has the perfect helicopter view of all that is faced, right? For some leaders, this may mean transcending othering to be truly open to stepping out of their comfort zone and really gaining from different perspectives.

Reducing the Other

I hadn't heard the term "othering" until about five years ago. Have you come across it? It's a way of differentiating or dividing an individual or group from another individual or group, *and* of attributing inferiority to the other. "The Others are perceived as objects who lack complexity, motivation, rationality and capabilities" (Kristeva 1994). So, we label "them" to confirm the legitimacy of our own views and define ourselves; they are tree huggers, nutcases, unreasonable, woke, nut jobs, an inferior race/gender/generation, difficult to work with, thus helping to define our place within *our* tribe (Pasini 2019). Subconsciously, we do it all the time—but it is to our own detriment. We miss the opportunity to "widen our gaze" to diverse perspectives that are critical for enhancing our understanding of a given context and subsequently, our decision making and innovative solutions. What often obstructs our ability to move beyond this are the biases or blind spots embedded in our worldviews (Wildman and Inayatullah 1996).

Dr. Dorough put her advice to you so beautifully. "It's always better to work directly with the people who are being impacted than if you don't—then you're really screwed, right? Legal exposure is created the moment that you choose not to talk to Indigenous people. Choosing to open your mind and educate yourself about the developments that have emerged in the way of Indigenous knowledge—in the way of understanding the world—outside of the values that have framed your perspectives, is a good thing."

The benefits from working with stakeholders can be profound. "Almost 50 years ago, Inuit were talking about the need for a comprehensive Arctic policy. We were talking about the need for coordination among the Arctic states and our direct involvement, to ensure that we safeguard the Arctic in a way that responds to our needs and those of others. Now the entire world community's focused on the Arctic largely because of the crisis of climate change."

> What I'm trying to say is that, if there were a genuine understanding of sustainable development, if we can find that equilibrium, it's to everyone's benefit. Imagine a world of 8.3 billion people who believed in sustainable development in the way that you and I do—giving care and receiving care. Wow, it'd be amazing!

So, as confronting—or uncomfortable—as it might be, taking a more integrated—indeed, curious—view is good for business and for the leader. To be able to do that successfully requires connecting what may feel disparate. Both–And.

Holding the Space—Bridging the Gap

As a leader who may face the need for collective leadership in order to find a strategic way forward in response to wicked opportunities, it is not only you who may need to come to terms with difference(s) in opinions or perspectives. Have you ever been in the situation when, say, you've watched members of your team trying to resolve an issue, but from different perspectives? Sometimes, it can feel like an out of body experience watching as the situation can get out of hand. Intensely and quickly, I've witnessed plenty of those!

Consequently, leaders like you need to be able to bridge different views, holding a safe space for all concerned so that they feel valued and respected—co-creating with dignity and empathy. Bridging, metaphorically, is a two-way means of creating a path across that which otherwise divides people (Küpers, Deeg, and Edwards 2015). It is hugely important and beneficial when it comes to regenerating lives, livelihoods, and the planet. By transcending othering, you create an environment of openness to opposing worldviews. This not only removes the problematic responses that we otherwise experience regularly but also enables those "aha" moments—the epiphanies required—if leaders and their organizations are to deal with their intractable problems (Küpers et al. 2015).

I don't want to undersell how challenging bridging can be. When an individual is confined within one paradigm, it can be difficult to have the capability to compare diverse paradigms or perspectives. But I also do not wish to undersell what a critical skill it is to be able to "hold the in-between spaces." Current adverse leadership practices can be transcended at those fluid points of intersection where the expected tensions and disruptions are transformed into new understandings and actions (Orton and Withrow 2015).

Taking a "helicopter" view to explore the issues from different perspectives and explore the "in between" spaces is vital for breakthroughs. Bridging requires valuing all perspectives as being independent, coherent, and having worth (Küpers et al. 2015). It requires a mix of much that we have discussed, particularly Li's (2016) "both–*and*" conceptualization, but also emotional intelligence and the appropriate strategic and ecosystems thinking. Nada from EcoPeace observed that "We try to emphasize the issues that bring us together more than focusing on what makes us different. So, we have reached a level where we can do some compromises, here and there, and still respect all of these differences."

Judging can be so easy to happen, right? But the benefits of "letting go" are huge.

Make the Peace

Nada also highlighted how important it is that, when bridging the disparate, we find and respect commonalities. While some constructive conflict is good for these discussions, keeping the diverse together requires leaders to be peacemakers. While this isn't a skill that is often raised as being important for leaders, I feel that with the momentous and turbulent change we are experiencing, in a world of declining trust and increasing outrage, we all need a lot of the peacemaker in us.

Nelson Mandela had a real mastery over his peacemaking skills. He was highly task focused and yet, attentive toward the feelings of others, seeing the best in humanity (Lieberfeld 2003). I have always found it extraordinary that Mandela was supposed to have had such a lack of bitterness toward those who imprisoned him. I have seen that in leaders where the best hold no malice but instead compassionately understand another's perspective.

I had the real privilege of spending time being trained by one of the "fathers of peace practice," Norwegian Johan Galtung. He must have worked with national and regional leaders across the globe who would have been viewed as evil or wrong. Yet, he did not view them that way. He saw their humanity. And just as Yana saw, Johan also emphasized the importance of a sense of humor when it comes to peacemaking. It can be so powerful in reducing destructive tensions.

For me, this also reiterates the importance of some of the facets of emotional intelligence that the leaders we have heard from in this book have discussed; namely, compassion, empathy, humility, and taking the time and interest to understand the other. It also means being genuine or respectful how you lead.

Yearning for Integrity

A section on integrity, really, should be a complete waste of your time. Yet, there is a need for me to passionately advocate for it. We need so much better from too many leaders.

Earlier in the book when I mentioned Volkswagen, Enron, and an array of other businesses, I hope that you realized at the time that I was bemoaning the dearth of ethical behavior, a lack of integrity in many. This is a significant issue, and I am not just talking about for society, although the stories that I could tell you about the impacts on communities and the natural environment resulting from unethical leaders and organizations are many. While it appears to be an issue rapidly dismissed by organizations and their leaders, the resulting decline in trust and organizational reputation has a huge array of adverse consequences for organizations—all of which take a long time to rectify. *Why* is there a proliferation of such stories?

While leaders may behave without integrity due to the pressures of delivering shareholder value or government policy, even in the medium term, there are no benefits to the organization. It really is as simple as that! If you hadn't realized it yet, people really are more sophisticated, educated, and coordinated than ever before. They can easily smell BS or spin offered with respect to the impacts of business and government on lives, livelihoods, and the planet. This is a key reason why so many sustainability programs, for that matter, are viewed with cynicism. It is so obvious!

The final thing that I will say is this: each of the leaders that I had the privilege to interview for this book got me thinking that a lack of integrity and ethics is often associated with a lack of emotional intelligence—a lack of respect for the individual, the group, the organization, the society, or the planet. On the flip side, each of the leaders interviewed had emotional intelligence in spades—empathy, humility, and curiosity spring to mind. And each of them was very strategic and tactical; indeed, they were tremendously successful.

It's vital that we have leaders who are transparent with others about what their strengths and limitations are (Cashman 2017). Borne out of enhanced self-awareness, such leaders are comfortable with sharing leadership and collaboration in general in order to confront the storm and indeed, various goals within the SDGs. They can deal with possibly the biggest challenge for leaders, the ability to be vulnerable.

The Courage to Not Know

For any leader to accept that they do not have all the answers, as is the case with our wicked problems (or opportunities), that push us to a deeper level of vulnerability can be downright scary (obviously!). It is scary because leadership, historically, has often been associated with very masculine attributes such as strength, confidence, and certainty—but also perhaps, borne out of fear or hurt (Brecher 2017). And vulnerability—being tender, questioning with interest, empathy, and flexibility—isn't one of them.

"Strong" leadership may provide security to followers, but it does not enable approachability nor comfort in sharing alternate views and insights. Insights that may better inform decision makers to make, well, better decisions that are more appropriate to the context in which they find themselves in—all vital when confronting the storm.

Hence, with all that we are experiencing across the globe, we need leaders who are open to vulnerability. I don't see it as a weakness, rather it takes real strength. Vulnerability requires a leader to be open to ideas other than your own, accepting uncertainty in the moment and recognizing, primarily, that you have limits—and that's okay when it leaves you emotionally exposed (Brecher 2017; Brown 2018).

This may leave you feeling uncomfortable, but really, what is the alternative? Conventional thinking just won't be enough. And where will that leave your organization, otherwise? It doesn't bear thinking sometimes. Yana put it best when she observed that her "work requires courage and almost being comfortable ensuring vulnerability. A vulnerability that comes with admitting that as a leader, I won't always have all the answers."

And then, there is Zainab.

"I believe that people think that gender-based violence only affects particular individuals, you know." That is something that Zainab has somehow been able to powerfully discuss with women audiences, sometimes with 1,000 present. Through her vulnerability, she enables others to reclaim hope and personal power. In Kenya. In Colombia.

Or, in Mali where she sat with a woman who struggled to talk about her terrible experience. "So, I put my arm around her, and I got her to sit near me on the couch. And then some of the women started talking. As soon as the women were talking, she started talking. And she was like in a trance. She explained how it happened to her when she was younger. 'I couldn't go to school because every time I black out. I get this attack. And then I have to wake up in hospital.' You know, David, this is unbelievable.

As she was talking, she was leaning on me. By the time I knew what happened, she blacked out."

I'm getting very emotional remembering this conversation with her.

"Gender-based violence," observed Zainab, "has no geographical boundary. It doesn't have any religious boundary. It affects both Muslims and Christians, educated, and illiterate. I think that's one of the most important things people need to understand: that it has no barrier. As women, we always think 'it is my fault'. That's the other thing you need to understand. The stigma is on us—not on the abuser. People are very reluctant to talk."

So many women have been deeply affected by, and appreciative of, Zainab sharing her own difficult, yet powerfully inspiring, story. Such vulnerability that she displays.

I was Minister of Foreign Affairs when I was going through serious, serious abuse. We think that because you've been this powerful person you don't experience these things. That's why it's very difficult to deal with it because women suffer in silence. So, I said to them, 'This is an issue that affects everybody'. And I gave them my experience. What I went through. What it caused me. How it affected me. You know, everybody was shocked. The best gift you can give to somebody who's going through a lot of pain is to share your own pain. You're sharing with them your vulnerability. When you're dealing with people, you also need them to understand that you're also vulnerable. You're a human being.

So don't be ashamed of it. Don't be afraid. This is what's happened to me. Well, today I am standing up. I was able to beat it. I succeeded.

When dealing with the storm, "you also have to get the people to see your vulnerability," she continued. "I think it's extremely important not to forget that because they treat leaders in a very different way. I always find a way to connect because that connection is what breaks down the barriers. When you are a leader, get them to understand you're also a person. You're an individual. You make mistakes. You have challenges."

I just have so much admiration for her.

This, therefore, compels me to come back to the need for emotional intelligence and a deep appreciation to accept that leadership needs to regenerate in the age of uncertainty as we continue to confront the storm. We certainly need to be more mindful toward the other, their emotions and views, and see them as being vital contributors to overcoming the storm. But perhaps, more importantly, to be able to overcome the storm, we need to understand ourselves and how we have held a glorious future back.

Drawing on emotional intelligence and an openness to different thinking, collaborating, doing, and becoming, regenerative leadership will allow informed clarity of the "in-between" connection between a preferred future and the present. This is facilitated by a greater understanding of ourselves and the interconnected world that we live in and a desire to create shared meaning and value—and hope.

Reflections

What did you make of the Indigenous worldview that meaning comes from the relationship (i) between people and the land and (ii) those among people, themselves?

On reflection, is it easy for you to understand the needs and values of others? Or do you unwittingly "other" them (i.e., downplay the importance of their views or insights)?

Think of a time when you led bringing the seemingly disparate together. How did that feel? Did that help your organization, strategically? What did you learn about those moments?

Do you act and communicate in ways that are reflective of just who you are? Even when you find yourself in a tough situation?

How do you feel that you serve your staff, stakeholders, and the planet?

Do you admit when you are uncertain how to tackle an issue?

– **CHAPTER 9** –

AND THEN,
THERE'S JUST YOU

You cannot get through a single day without having an impact on the world around you. What you do makes a difference, and you have to decide what kind of a difference you want to make.

Jane Goodall

And Then, There's Just You

It's been such a privilege for me to introduce you to: John; Zainab; Diego and David; Gidon, Yana, and Nada; Dr. Brundtland; Daniel and Milena; Eva; Dr. Zhou; Dr. Dorough; and Oren. They each have such amazing and inspiring insights. I hope that you enjoyed reading their insights and got as much out of those conversations as I did.

Yet, this book wasn't about them or their stories. It was about you. This book has always been about you. It was borne out of a passion to serve *you*; to help you deal confidently with the anticipated bumps, shocks, and crises as your own story continues to unfold.

Looking Backward

If you've rarely had anything to do with social, economic, or environmental issues (apart from the pandemic), I really hope that my thoughts—as well as the insights gained from the true leaders that we've heard from—have created a sense of urgency and inspiration for you.

I'd always felt that referring to these issues as "sustainability" issues didn't do them justice. It didn't do justice to the scale of them, nor how adverse the impacts associated with them can be. Sustainability was about maintaining business as usual. You may recall in the Preface, for example, that I tried to convey the horror of Australia's 2019/2020 "black summer" fires. That was something I witnessed first-hand and it left me shaken—and yet there have since been similar terrifying fires on the west coast of the United States and Canada in locations that rarely experience significant forest fires. As I write this, I have just read a BBC article observing that "Zhengzhou saw 624 mm of rainfall on Tuesday, with a third of that amount falling between 16:00 and 17:00 alone, which smashed historical records" (BBC 2021). And that conveys what we can expect solely from climate change—let alone all the other social and environmental issues that are facing us today.

So that is why I referred to the storm. To convey the power of what we face.

And yet, the speed of change that we are experiencing in a networked world—and the frequency with which we are experiencing momentous and turbulent events—just magnifies the problems.

I observed that our worldviews, reflective of our stories, change slowly in response to external change. Stories have power. They create meaning for each of us and facilitate the organization of us as individuals and groups. However, stories are just that—*stories*. Stories that may have had a truth to them in centuries past but have not been modified in response to new circumstances have little merit. They are like an echo from the past—a glorious past that has anchored us, but now risks dragging us down.

Looking Forward—and Outward

Yet, in the face of the storm, leaders like you have significant opportunities. Opportunities to better manage the risks and be able to ride out the bumps, shocks, and crises more successfully. Opportunities to enhance your organization's services, products, brand, or reputation. Just look at the opportunities that Daniel and Milena are accessing in the Unreasonable Group, that Eva is accessing in Houdini or those that Diego and David from the Latin American Leadership Academy are accessing for their students in some of the direst situations imaginable.

If we are to confront the storm in this age of real uncertainty, we need to confront our stories. Our stories of how a leader needs to act. The critical issues we face need leaders to take a more holistic perspective and take a more collaborative approach to the storm. That means being mindful that leaders have a blind spot that must be confronted, as Senge, Scharmer, and Jaworski (2007) observe. It has nothing to do with "the what and how—not what leaders do and how they do it—but the *who*: who we are and the inner place ... from which we operate, both individually and collectively. That means letting go of old identities and old stories and being open beyond your preconceptions" (Senge et al. 2007). It means being open to learning from, for example, the worldviews and stories that Dalee and Oren shared with us. By doing so, we reduce the obstacles in ourselves that may prohibit us from accessing those opportunities.

Just before we wrap up, I didn't share with you something that Dr. Zhou had said to me on this point. Right at the end of our conversation, I was so touched by his passion and obvious belief when he said:

> We are facing great emergencies. Climate emergency. Biodiversity emergency. Public health emergency. Great challenges. We need to work together. It needs collective, global action. We in China need to learn from Western countries as well as Western countries may want to learn from us. This is a time to adopt, to accept, to tolerate as we need to work together to fight COVID-19, to fight climate change; we need to work together.

Isn't that belief scalable to you on an institutional level? Isn't that possible for *all* leaders—knowing that, as Diego, David, Daniel, Milena, and Eva passionately highlighted, there are huge opportunities? Even in Africa or the Middle East, in the harshest of situations, Zainab, Gidon, Yana, and Nada are passionate about collaborating to continue delivering opportunities for regenerating lives, livelihoods, and the planet.

Now, you may have some critical thoughts about the key skills and traits discussed in the previous pages. That's okay. Please feel free to e-mail your feedback to me at David.Ross@phoenixstrategic.com.au. I am extremely aware that the framework is just a starting point and I love trying to enhance the framework through time, based on what I learn from readers who have engaged with it.

To reiterate: the skills and traits across the four segments are not separate. They are interlocked; they reinforce one another. The key reason for the framework is to underline that the old ways of thinking, doing, and being are often no longer appropriate—and, as Brene Brown put it, it's also to remind us that "where we're faced with seemingly intractable challenges and a seismic need for innovation, we now need braver leaders" (Brown 2018).

It's brave leaders that we need. Who dare to question the current approaches and stories.

Who, through their thinking, connecting, doing, and becoming, offer hope.

And who rise above looking inward to develop more and more leaders—the Team of 5 Million *or* 5 Billion—who are ready to be sincere in confronting the storm.

Brave leaders like you.

Thanks so much for your time and interest.

Reflections

What does the world look like for you and your organization in 10 years' time? What is the glorious future? How will its purpose, mission, and core values have changed?

What could be your organization's story going forward? And your own story?

If you need to take a staged approach to integrating a regenerative mindset into your organization, what would that look like?

How will you lead the future?

What skills and traits do you believe will be vital for yourself and your organization in confronting the storm?

What is an image that conveys for you what leadership needs to look like?

Who do you serve?

What will your legacy be?

Collated Reflections

Chapter 1

As you progress through the reflections at the end of each chapter, please grab a pad and pen and *take your time*.

What has change looked like, or felt like, for you over the past two years? Over the past five years? What change if any have you noticed with respect to:

- Your local, national, and global economy? Is the makeup of industries changing? Are the industries or companies that dominated five years ago still dominant?
- Social issues? Have new social issues or movements risen? What is being questioned or confronted regarding once taken-for-granted values and beliefs?
- Technology? Are you seeing at least some of what Kurzweil wrote about?
- Environmental issues? What environmental issues are now a strategic risk for your organization? Does your risk register need revision?

What implications does this kind of change have for your organization? Or you? Does it feel like change is speeding up? Similar to what Zainab said about Africa, does your organization feel vulnerable?

How has your organization responded to wicked problems?

Have you worked in an organization that was focused on a glorious past? What did that look like? What did leadership in the organization look like?

Chapter 2

What is the dominant story about leadership in your organization? Does it reflect 20th-century thinking? Is that appropriate as we experience momentous change?

What does sustainability or CSR look like in your organization? Is it an awkward, greenwashed add-on solely for short-term profits?

Has *genuine* value been placed within your organization on lives, livelihoods, and the planet? Has sustainability or CSR helped your organization maintain a sterling reputation?

Consider your organization's culture. What are the prevalent worldviews and values? How do these influence decisions around lives, livelihoods, and the planet?

Do you think that level of exasperation is only "localized" to Latin America? What do you see with your own organization? Is conflict "waiting" for you?

How do you think that momentous change could impact dominant worldviews in your organization? Could they change at all?

Ask yourself, "What does my worldview look like? How do I respond to the worldviews of others?"

Chapter 3

What do you want your organization's reputation to look like or to be perceived? What should the organization and your leadership be remembered for?

Is dealing with wicked problems a core competence within your organization?

What *genuine* contributions would your key stakeholders perceive your organization has made to improving lives and livelihoods and regenerating the planet?

If you have led your organization during a time that it was subjected to stakeholder outrage, what behavior was exhibited by you or your staff toward the outraged "other"?

If you *had to* lead your organization while it was subjected to stakeholder outrage, what would you do? What behaviors would be required?

Dr. Brundtland shared her thoughts on what is holding leaders back with respect to regenerating lives, livelihoods, and the planet. What do you think is holding leaders back?

Chapter 4

Houle observed that "new and future realities are rushing in everywhere ... the old (order) holds on, but is gasping and failing." Has that shown itself in your sector? If so, how?

What does growth look like at present within your industry or as supported by your government? As Gibbons observes, is it (un)sustainable?

Is incrementalism your organization's mantra when dealing with our wicked problems?

How could your organization experience disruption or its own "Kodak moment"? Is there the risk of organizational brittleness?

What could regenerative thinking look like for you?

Where have you seen leaders who mirrored Greenleaf's servant-style leaders who go "beyond one's self-interest"? What did that look like? How did it benefit others or an organization?

As a leader in this context faced, what do you think that you need to *be*?

Chapter 5

How does your organization ensure that the "nestedness" that Hahn and Tampe referred to is incorporated into strategic—or event tactical—decision making?

What role could influencers play in your organization with respect to enhancing lives, livelihoods, and the planet?

What assumptions are you bringing to thinking and decision making, conscious, or otherwise? What lessons have you taken away from the impact these have had on resulting decisions and outcomes?

What sources of information do you call on to help with understanding your context?

What means do you call on to unearth individual or organizational blind spots?

Chapter 6

Who could you involve in developing more informed strategies? What could that look like?

Would your organization's executive leaders be receptive to collaborating with middle managers? What does that say about the dominant leadership styles?

How do you create the safe space necessary for conversations of such importance?

How do you react in a situation when you do not have the expertise? Are you open to new and innovative ideas and approaches, *particularly when they are not your own*?

What does emotional intelligence look like to you?

How do you feel that your own leadership story informs your understanding of your own behavior or that of other's?

Do you try to view things from another's perspective?

How do you behave toward others when things are not going well, are uncertain, or tense? Why do you believe that many leaders have a need to control situations? Is it borne from here? Or something else?

When you listen to others, do you listen *deeply*?

Chapter 7

What's your organization's story, currently and historically? What does it mean? What should you do now?

Who do you involve when you need to make sense of what the current situation is and what it means? Are you open to widely different views like Dr. Zhou?

What assumptions do you have about the future? What implications does that have for your organization? And how do you manage these assumptions?

Do you feel that you are a leader that "leans into disruption," exploring where there is an opportunity and/or need to adapt? Do you do so in a brisk, even collaborative, manner? What does that look like?

How do you or your team view contradictions? Are the negatives associated with a context ignored and isolated from the focus? What has this meant for the quality of strategies delivered? How could the positives and negatives be better contemplated, holistically?

Are you a firefighter? Or do you have laser-like focus? What does this mean for how you operate in an age of uncertainty?

Do you readily bounce back? What do you do to look after yourself? Do you have a clear sense of purpose?

Chapter 8

What did you make of the Indigenous worldview that meaning comes from the relationship (i) between people and the land and (ii) those among people, themselves?

On reflection, is it easy for you to understand the needs and values of others? Or do you unwittingly "other" them (i.e., downplay the importance of their views or insights)?

Think of a time when you led bringing the seemingly disparate together. How did that feel? Did that help your organization, strategically? What did you learn about those moments?

Do you act and communicate in ways that are reflective of just who you are? Even when you find yourself in a tough situation?

How do you feel that you serve your staff, stakeholders, and the planet?

Do you admit when you are uncertain how to tackle an issue?

Chapter 9

What does the world look like for you and your organization in 10 years' time? What is the glorious future? How will its purpose, mission, and core values have changed?

What could be your organization's story going forward? And your own story?

If you need to take a staged approach to integrating a regenerative mindset into your organization, what would that look like?

How will you lead the future?

What skills and traits do you believe will be vital for yourself and your organization in confronting the storm?

What is an image that conveys for you what leadership needs to look like?

Who do you serve?

What will your legacy be?

References

Chapter 1

Bennis, W., and B. Nanus. 1985. *Leaders: The strategies for taking charge.* NY: Harper and Row.

Bouée, C.E. 2013. *VUCA, Dao and Learning From China.* www.management-issues.com/opinion/6721/vuca-dao-and-learning-from-china/ (accessed June 13, 2020).

Camillus, J.C. May 2008. *Strategy as a Wicked Problem,* pp. 98–106. Harvard Business Review.

Cascio, J. 2020. *Facing the Age of Chaos.* Medium. https://medium.com/@cascio/facing-the-age-of-chaos-b00687b1f51d_(accessed July 27, 2020).

Directorate for Science, Technology, and Innovation, OECD. 2016. *An OECD Horizon Scan of Megatrends and Technology Trends in the Context of Future Research Policy.* Commissioned by the Danish Agency for Science, Technology and Innovation.

IEP. 2021. *Ecological Threat Report 2021: Understanding Ecological Threats, Resilience, and Peace.* Institute for Economics and Peace, Australia.

IPCC. 2022. *Climate Change 2022: Impacts, Adaptation and Vulnerability.* Intergovernmental Panel on Climate Change.

Johansen, B. 2007. *Get There Early.* CA: Berrett-Kohler Publishers Inc.

Kurzweil, R. 2006. *The Singularity Is Near: When Humans Transcend Biology.* NY: Penguin Books.

Morgan, T. 2020. "Solving the Wickedest Problem: Reconciling Different Worldviews." *Journal of Futures Studies* 24, no. 4, pp. 83–94.

Francis, P. 2015. *Laudato si: On Care for Our Common Home.* Encyclical.

Rittel, H.W.J., and M.M. Webber. June 1973. "Dilemmas in a General Theory of Planning." *Policy Sciences* 4, no. 2, pp. 155–169.

Ronfeldt, D. 1996. *Tribes, Institutions, Markets, Networks: A Framework About Societal Evolution.* CA: RAND Corporation.

Ronfeldt, D. 2016. *Materials for Two Theories: TIMN and STA:C.* http://twotheories.blogspot.com/2016/05/organizational-forms-compared-my.html (accessed June 11, 2020).

Roser, M. 2013. "Employment in Agriculture." *Our World in Data.* https://ourworldindata.org/employment-in-agriculture (accessed June 12, 2020).

Sambira, J. n.d. "'Take Away the Guns', Women Tell UN Envoy." *Africa Renewal.* www.un.org/africarenewal/web-features/%E2%80%98take-away-guns%E2%80%99-women-tell-un-envoy (accessed November 16, 2021).

Steffen, W., K. Richardson, J. Rockström, S.E. Cornell, I. Fetzer, E.M. Bennett, R. Biggs, S.R. Carpenter, W. de Vries, C. de Wit, C. Folke, D. Gerten, J. Heinke, G.M. Mace, L.M. Persson, V. Ramanathan, B. Reyers, and S. Sörlin. February 2015. "Planetary Boundaries: Guiding Human Development on a Changing Planet." *Science* 347, issue 6223, pp. 736–746.

UNDP. 2020. "Human Development Report 2020." *The Next Frontier: Human Development and the Anthropocene.* NY: United Nations Development Programme.

United Nations. 2019. *Sustainable Development Goals.* https://sustainabledevelopment.un.org/sdgs (accessed June 13, 2020).

Yarger, H. 2006. *Strategic Theory for the 21st Century: The Little Book on Big Strategy.* Strategic Studies Institute monograph, PA: US Army War College.

Chapter 2

Allio, R.J. 2007. "Bad Leaders: How They Get That Way and What to Do About Them." *Strategy and Leadership* 35, no. 3, pp. 12–17.

Camrass, K. 2020. "Regenerative Futures." *Foresight* 22, no. 4, pp. 401–415.

Carson, R. 1962. *Silent Spring.* MA: Houghton Mifflin Publishers.

Eidelson, R., and J. Eidelson. March, 2003. "Dangerous Ideas: Five Beliefs That Propel Groups Towards Conflict." *American Psychologist* 58, no. 3, pp. 182–192.

Fullerton, J. 2015. *Regenerative Capitalism: How Universal Principles and Patterns Will Shape Our New Economy.* Capital Institute.

Ganz, M. 2009. *Why Stories Matter.* https://commonslibrary.org/why-stories-matter-the-art-and-craft-of-social-change/ (accessed October 14, 2021).

Gibbons, L.V. July 2020. "Regenerative—The New Sustainable?" *Sustainability* 12, pp. 1–19.

Hahn, T., and M. Tampe. 2021. "Strategies for Regenerative Business." *Strategic Organization* 19, no. 3, pp. 456–477.

Kakabadse, A. January–February 2000. "From Individual to Team to Cadré: Tracking Leadership for the Third Millennium." *Strategic Change* 9, pp. 5–16.

Kurzweil, R. 2006. *The Singularity Is Near: When Humans Transcend Biology.* NY: Penguin Books.

LALA. 2021. *About Us: We Want to Change the Landscape of the Region.* Latin America Leadership Academy. www.latinamericanleadershipacademy.org/about (accessed October 06, 2021).

OECD. 2018. *A Broken Social Elevator? How to Promote Social Mobility.* Paris. OECD Publishing.

Ramos, J.M. 2003. "From Critique to Critical Recovery: Critical Futures Studies and Causal Layered Analysis." Australian Foresight Institute Monograph Series No. 2. VIC: Swinburne University.

Rarick. C.A. Autumn 2007. "The "Other" Art of War: Strategic Implications of Sun Pin's Bing Fa." *SAM Advanced Management Journal*, pp. 4–8.

Tibbs, H. March 2011. "Changing Cultural Values and the Transition to Sustainability." *Journal of Futures Studies* 15, no. 3, pp. 13–32.

UNDP. 2021. "Regional Human Development Report 2021." *Trapped: High Inequality and Low Growth in Latin America and the Caribbean.* NY: United Nations Development Programme.

Valk, J., S. Belding, A. Crumpton, N. Harter, and J. Ream. 2011. "Worldviews and Leadership: Thinking and Acting the Bigger Pictures." *Journal of Leadership Studies* 15, no. 2, pp. 54–63.

Wahl, D.C. 2018. "Sustainability Is Not Enough: We Need Regenerativ e Cultures." *Resilience.* www.resilience.org/stories/2018-05-23/sustainability-is-not-enough-we-need-regenerative-cultures/ (accessed June 25, 2020).

Chapter 3

Albrecht, G., G. Sartore, L. Connor, N. Higginbotham, S. Freeman, B. Kelly, H. Stain, A. Tonna, and G. Pollard. 2007. "Solstalgia: The Distress Caused by Environmental Change." *Australasian Psychiatry*, Vol. 15 Supplement.

Bennis, W., and B. Nanus. 1985. "Leaders: The Strategies for Taking Charge." NY: Harper and Row.

Brundtland, G. 1987. *Report of the World Commission on the Environment and Development: Our Common Future.* United Nations General Assembly document A/42/427.

Bussey, M. 2006. "Shadow Dancing: Colonizing Racisms and Their Discontents." *Journal of Futures Studies* 11, no. 2, pp. 101–118.

Edelman. 2022. "Edelman Trust Barometer." www.edelman.com/ (accessed January 28, 2022).

Elkington, J. 2020. *Green Swans: The Coming Boom in Regenerative Capitalism.* NY: Fast Company Press.

Holt, S., J. Macques, J. Hu, and A. Wood. January 2017. "Cultivating Empathy: New Perspectives on Educating Business Leaders." *The Journal of Values-Based Leadership* 10, Issue 1, pp. 1–25.

Houle, D. 2022. *A Look in 2022: A Split Screen Year.* David Houle and Associates.

Mukherjee, A.S. December 2016. *Why We're Seeing So Many Corporate Scandals.* https://hbr.org/2016/12/why-were-seeing-so-many-corporate-scandals (accessed July 31, 2020).

Rittel, H.W., and M.M. Webber. 1973. "Dilemmas in a General Theory of Planning." *Policy Sciences* 4, no. 2, pp. 155–169.

Ronfeldt, D. 2016. *Materials for Two Theories: TIMN and STA:C.* http:// twotheories.blogspot.com/2016/05/organizational-forms-compared-my .html (accessed June 11, 2020).

Tibbs, H. March 2011. "Changing Cultural Values and the Transition to Sustainability." *Journal of Futures Studies* 15, no. 3, pp.13–32.

World Bank. 2018. *Decline of Global Extreme Poverty Continues But Has Slowed: World Bank.* www.worldbank.org/en/news/press-release/2018/09/19/ decline-of-global-extreme-poverty-continues-but-has-slowed-world-bank (accessed July 31, 2020).

Zak, P. 2019. *How Our Brains Decide When to Trust.* Harvard Business Review. https://hbr.org/2019/07/how-our-brains-decide-when-to-trust (accessed July 30, 2020).

Chapter 4

Elkington, J. 2020. *Green Swans: The Coming Boom in Regenerative Capitalism.* NY: Fast Company Press.

Fullerton, J. 2015. *Regenerative Capitalism: How Universal Principles and Patterns Will Shape Our New Economy.* Capital Institute.

Garrido, L., D. Fazekas, H. Pollitt, A. Smith, M. Berg von Linde, M. McGregor, and M. Westphal. 2018. *Forthcoming Major Opportunities for Growth and Climate Action: A Technical Note.* A New Climate Economy contributing paper.

Gibbons, L.V. July 2020. "Regenerative—The New Sustainable?" *Sustainability* 12, pp. 1–19.

Greenleaf, R.K. 1970. *The Servant as Leader.* Greenleaf Publishing Center.

Hawkins, B., and G. Edwards. 2015. "Managing the Monsters of Doubt: Liminality, Threshold Concepts and Leadership Learning." *Management Learning* 46, no. 1, pp. 24–43.

Houle, D. 2022. *A Look in 2022: A Split Screen Year.* David Houle and Associates.

Kiker, D.S., J.S. Callahan, and M.B. Kiker. Summer 2019. "Exploring the Boundaries of Servant Leadership: A Meta-Analysis of the Main and Moderate Effects of Servant Leadership on Behavioral and Affective Outcomes." *Journal of Managerial Issues* 31, no. 2, pp. 172–197.

Orton, A., and L. Withrow. 2015. "Transformative Potentials of Liminal Leadership." *Journal of Religious Leadership* 14, no. 1, pp. 23–44.

Pekerti, A.A., and S. Sendjaya. April 2010. "Exploring Servant Leadership Across Cultures: Comparative Study in Australian and Indonesia." *The International Journal of Human Resource Management* 21, no. 5, pp. 754–780.

Reeves, M., S. Levin, and D. Ueda. January–February 2016. *The Biology of Corporate Survival: Natural Ecosystems Hold Surprising Lessons for Survival,* pp. 47–55. Harvard Business Review.

Sroufe, R. 2017. "Integration and Organizational Change Towards Sustainability." *Journal of Cleaner Production* 162, pp. 315–329.

UNDP. 2020. "Human Development Report 2020.*" The Next Frontier: Human Development and the Anthropocene*. NY: United Nations Development Programme.

Winston, B., and D. Fields. 2015. "Seeking and Measuring the Essential Behaviors of Servant Leadership." *Leadership and Organizational Development Journal* 36, no. 4, pp. 413–434.

Chapter 5

Berglund, J. April 2020. "After Fukushima: Safety Culture and Fostering Critical Thinking." *Safety Science* 124, pp. 1–6.

Butler, H.A. 2012. "Halpern Critical Thinking Assessment Predicts Real-World Outcomes of Critical Thinking." *Applied Cognitive Psychology* 26, no. 5, pp. 721–729.

Ennis, R.H. Summer 1993. "Critical Thinking Assessment." *Theory Into Practice* 32, no. 3, pp. 179–186.

Gallis, M., and H. Millar. Autumn 2006. "Human Systems and Ecosystems: We Need a Different Way of Thinking." *American Forestry*, pp. 18–24.

Hahn, T., and M. Tampe. 2021. "Strategies for Regenerative Business." *Strategic Organization* 19, no. 3, pp. 456–477.

Heracleous, L. 1998. "Strategic Thinking or Strategic Planning?" *Long Range Planning* 31, no. 3, pp. 481–487.

Herrero, L. 2010. *Changing the Way We Think About Change: How Does Viral Change™ Work?* https://viralchange.files.wordpress.com/2010/03/changing-the-way-we-think-about-change-leandro-herrero.pdf (accessed November 30, 2021).

Holtström, J., C. Bjellerup, and J. Eriksson. 2019. "Business Model Development for Sustainable Apparel Consumption." *Journal of Strategy and Management* 12, no. 4, pp. 481–504.

Houdini. 2018. *This is Houdini: Planetary Boundaries Assessment 2018*. https://houdinisportswear.com/en-gl/sustainability/planetary-boundaries-assessment (accessed May 16, 2021).

Houdini. 2021. *How We Want to Change the World*. https://houdinisportswear.com/en-gl/sustainability/how-we-want-to-change-the-world (accessed July 09, 2021)

Housman, J. 2020. "Houdini Sportswear Has a Blueprint for Escaping the Gear Pollution Treadmill." *Adventure Journal*. www.adventure-journal.com/2020/09/houdini-sportswear-has-a-blueprint-for-escaping-the-gear-pollution-treadmill/ (accessed July 10, 2021).

Longobardi, D. 2004. "Thinking About Ecosystems." *American Banker* 169, issue 34.

Milojević, I., and S. Inayatullah. January 2021. "Narrative Foresight and Covid-19: Successes and Failures in Managing the Pandemic." *Journal of Futures Studies*. https://jfsdigital.org/2021/01/21/narrative-foresight-and-covid-19-successes-and-failures-in-managing-the-pandemic/ (accessed June 22, 2021).

Shank, M., and M. Bédat. 2020. "Analysis: Fast Fashion Comes at a Steep Price for the Environment." *MSNBC*. www.msnbc.com/msnbc/analysis-fast-fashion-comes-steep-price-the-environment-msna852631 (accessed July 10, 2021).

Shaw, A., O.L. Liu, L. Gu, E. Kardonova, I. Chirikov, G. Li, S. Hu, N. Yu, L. Ma, F. Guo, Q. Su, J. Shi, H. Shi, and P. Loyolka. 2020. "Thinking Critically and Critical Thinking: Validating the Russian HEIghten® *critical Thinking Assessment."* *Studies in Higher Education* 45, no. 9, pp. 1933–1948.

Wright, N. August 2018. "Strategic Thinking: Deal With the Stuff That Comes After Strategic Planning." *Public Management*, pp. 8–11.

Yarger, H. 2006. *Strategic Theory for the 21st Century: The Little Book on Big Strategy*. Strategic Studies Institute monograph. PA: US Army War College.

Chapter 6

Archer, D., and A. Cameron. June 2012. *Collaborative Leadership*. www.trainingjournal.com

Baggio, G., M. Qadir, and V. Smakhtin. 2021. "Freshwater Availability Status Across Countries for Human and Ecosystem Needs." *Science of the Total Environment* 792, pp. 1–11.

Clampitt, P.G. 2016. *Communicating for Managerial Effectiveness*. WI: Sage Publishing. Sixth edition.

Duff, S. May 2017. "Empathy in Leadership." *Training Journal*, pp. 9–11.

EcoPeace ME. 2020. *About Us*. https://old.ecopeaceme.org/ecopeace/about-us/ (accessed December 30, 2020).

El-Anis, I. and R. Smith. 2013. "Freshwater Security, Conflict and Cooperation: The Case of the Red Sea-Dead Sea Conduit Project." *Journal of Developing Societies* 29, no. 1, pp. 1–22.

Fischhendler, I., and D. Katz. 2013. "The Impact of Uncertainties on Cooperation Over Transboundary Water: The Case of Israeli-Palestinian Negotiations." *Geoforum* 50, pp. 200–210.

Gemmill, G., and J. Oakley. 1992. "Leadership: An Alienating Social Myth?" *Human Relations* 45, no. 2, pp. 113–129.

George, J.M. 2000. "Emotions and Leadership: The Role of Emotional Intelligence." *Human Relations* 53, no. 8, pp. 1027–1055.

Goleman, D., R. Boyatzis, and A. McKee. 2002. *Primal Leadership Learning to Lead With Emotional Intelligence.* MA: Harvard Business Press.

Greenwood, S. Summer 2014. "Water Security, Climate Change and Governance in the Arab World." *Middle East Policy* 21, no. 2, pp. 140–156.

Hambrick, D.C., and J.W. Fredrickson. November 2001. "Are You Sure You Have a Strategy?" *Academy of Management* 15, no. 4, pp. 48–59.

He, W., P. Hao, X. Huang, L. Long, N.J. Hiller, and S. Li. 2020. "Different Roles of Shared and Vertical Leadership in Promoting Team Creativity: Cultivating and Synthesizing Team Members' Individual Creativity." *Personnel Psychology* 73, pp. 199–225.

Holt, S., J. Marques, J. Hu, and A. Wood. 2017. "Cultivating Empathy: New Perspectives on Educating Business Leaders." *The Journal of Values-Based Leadership*, Vol. 10: Iss. 1, Article 3.

IPCC. 2022. *Climate Change 2022: Impacts, Adaptation and Vulnerability.* Intergovernmental Panel on Climate Change.

Kania, J., and M. Kramer. 2011. *Collective Impact.* Stanford Social Innovation Review. Winter edition. https://ssir.org/articles/entry/collective_impact (accessed July 14, 2021).

Kukenberger, M.R., and D. D'Innocenzo. 2020. "The Building Blocks of Shared Leadership: The Interactive Effects of Diversity Types, Team Climate and Time." *Personnel Psychology* 73, pp. 125–150.

Morrison, E., S. Hutchesons, E. Nilsen, J. Fadden, and N. Franklin. 2019. *Strategic Doing: Ten Skills for Agile Leadership.* NJ: John Wiley & Sons Inc.

Ross, D., B. Leonard, and S. Inayatullah. 2021. "Leadership Beyond the Great Pause: Climate Change and Other Wicked Problems." *Journal of Futures Studies.* https://jfsdigital.org/leadership-beyond-the-great-pause-climate-change-and-other-wicked-problems/

Schein, J.S. 2009. *Emotional Intelligence for Dummies.* John Wiley and Sons, Canada.

Stibbe, D., D. Prescott, The Partnering Initiative, and UNDESA. 2020. *The SDG Partnership Guidebook: A Practical Guide to Building High-Impact Multi-Stakeholder Partnerships for the Sustainable Development Goals.* UN and The Partnering Initiative.

Wisse, B., D. Rus, A.C. Keller, and E. Sleebos. 2019. "'Fear of Losing Power Corrupts Those Who Wield It': The Combined Effects of Leader Fear of Losing Power and Competitive Climate on Leader Self-Serving Behavior." *European Journal of Work and Organizational Psychology* 28, no. 6, pp. 742–755.

Chapter 7

Chebbi, H., D. Yahlaoul, D. Vrontis, and A. Thrassou. 2017. "Ambidextrous Leadership on the Internalization of Emerging Market Firms: The Case of India." *Thunderbird International Business Review* 59, no. 3, pp. 421–436.

Christianson, M.K., and M.A. Barton. March 2021. "Sensemaking in the Time of Covid-19." *Management Studies* 58, no. 2, pp. 572–576.

Denning, S. 2015. "Agile: It's Time to Put It to Use to Manage Business Complexity." *Strategy & Leadership* 43, no. 5, pp. 10–17.

Hahn, T., and M. Tampe. 2021. "Strategies for Regenerative Business." *Strategic Organization* 19, no. 3, pp. 456–477.

Holst, A. February 2021. *Volume of Data, Information Created, Captured, Copied, and Consumed Worldwide From 2010 to 2024.* www.statista.com/statistics/871513/worldwide-data-created/ (accessed March 12, 2021).

Horney, N., W. Passmore, and T. O'Shea. 2010. "Leadership Agility: A Business Imperative for a VUCA World." *People and Strategy* 33, issue 4, pp. 32–38.

Inayatullah, S. 2008. "Six Pillars: Futures Thinking for Transforming." *Foresight* 10, no. 1, pp. 4–21.

Smith, C.L. 2017. "Coaching for Leadership Resilience: An Integrated Approach." *International Coaching Psychology Review* 12, no. 1, pp. 6–23.

O'Driscoll, T., and J. Bleak. 2013. *CEO Insights From the Front Lines of the Business Supernova.* Duke Corporate Education. www.dukece.com/insights/ceo-insightsfrom-front-lines-business-supernova/ (accessed March 03, 2021).

O'Reilly, C.A., and M.L. Tushman. April 2004. "The Ambidextrous Organization." *Harvard Business Review* 82, no. 4, pp. 74–81.

Pievani, T. 2014. "The Sixth Mass Extinction: Anthropocene and the Human Impact on Biodiversity." *Rend. Fis. Acc. Lincei* 25, pp. 85–93.

Seligman, M.E.P. April 2011. "Building Resilience." *Harvard Business Review*, pp. 100–106.

Smith, W. K., and M.W. Lewis. 2011. "Toward a Theory of Paradox: A Dynamic Equilibrium Model of Organizing." *Academy of Management Review* 36, pp. 381–403.

Tadmor, C.T., Y. Hong, M.M. Chao, F Wiruchnipawan, and W. Wang. 2012. "Multicultural Experiences Reduce Intergroup Bias Through Epistemic Unfreezing." *Journal of Personality and Social Psychology* 103, no. 5, p. 750.

Tilman, D., M. Clark, D.R. Williams, K. Kimmel, S. Polasky, and C. Packer. June 2017. "Future Threats to Biodiversity and Pathways to Their Prevention." *Nature* 546, pp. 73–81.

van der Laan, L. August 2008. "The Imperative of Strategic Foresight to Strategic Thinking." *Journal of Futures Studies* 13, no. 1, pp. 21–42.

Weick, K., K.M. Sutcliffe, and D. Obstfeld. July–August 2005. "Organizing and the Process of Sensemaking." *Organization Science* 16, no. 4, pp. 409–421.

Zhang, Y., D.A. Waldman, Y. Han, and B. Li. 2015. "Paradoxical Leader Behaviors in People Management: Antecedents and Consequences." *Academy of Management Journal* 58, no. 2, pp. 538–566.

Chapter 8

Baggio, G., M. Qadir, and V. Smakhtin. 2021. "Freshwater Availability Status Across Countries for Human and Ecosystem Needs." *Science of the Total Environment* 792, pp. 1–11.

Begay, J. June 2021. *An Indigenous Systems Approach to the Climate Crisis.* Stanford Social Innovation Review. https://ssir.org/ (accessed June 24, 2021).

Brecher, N. January 2017. "Are Leadership and Vulnerability at Odds?" *Journal of Property Management* 82, no. 1, p. 23.

Brown, B. 2018. *Dare to Lead.* Penguin Random House, UK.

Cashman, K. 2017. "Deepening Authenticity for Sustainable Leadership." *Leadership Excellence Essentials*, no. 2, pp. 38–39.

Dorough, D.S. September 21, 2021. *The Ripples We Feel: UN Must Respect, Honor Indigenous Peoples' Role.* Anchorage Daily News.

Forte, V. 2019. "A Review of 21 Lessons for the 21st Century." *Journal of Business Ethics* 21, pp. 33–48.

Graham, M. 2008. "Some Thoughts About the Philosophical Underpinnings of Aboriginal Worldviews." *Australian Humanities Review*, Iss. 45, pp. 181–194.

Harari, Y.N. 2011. *Sapiens: A Brief History of Humankind.* Penguin Random House, UK.

ICC. 2021. *Inuit: United Voice of the Arctic.* www.inuitcircumpolar.com/ (accessed December 09, 2021).

IPCC. 2022. *Climate Change 2022: Impacts, Adaptation and Vulnerability.* Intergovernmental Panel on Climate Change.

Kennedy, A., C. McGouran, and J. Kemper. 2020. "Alternate Paradigms for Sustainability: The Maori Worldview." *European Journal of Marketing* 54, no. 4, pp. 825–855.

Kristeva, J. 1994. *Strangers to Ourselves.* NY, Columbia University Press. Cited in W. Krumer-Küpers, J. Deeg, and M. Edwards. September 2015. "'Inter-Bridging' Bridges and Bridging as Metaphors for 'Syn-Integrality' in Organization Studies and Practice." *Integral Review* 11, no. 3, pp. 117–137.

Li, P.P. 2016. "Global Implications of the Indigenous Epistemological System From the East: How to Apply Yin-Yang Balancing to Paradox Management." *Cross Cultural & Strategic Management* 23, no. 1, pp. 42–77.

Lieberfeld, D. July 2003. "Nelson Mandela: Partisan and Peacemaker." *Negotiation Journal*, pp. 229–250.

Lopez, B. 2007. "The Leadership Imperative: An Interview With Oren Lyons." *Manoa* 19, no. 2, pp. 4–12.

Morgan, T. 2020. "Solving the Wickedest Problem: Reconciling Differing Worldviews." *Journal of Futures Studies* 24, no. 4, pp. 83–94.

Orton, A., and L. Withrow. 2015. "Transformational Potentials of Liminal Leadership." *Journal of Religious Leadership* 23, no. 1, pp. 23–44.

Pasini, M. 2019. "An Introduction to the Proceedings of the Conference "Us' vs. 'Them': The Rhetoric of 'Othering' From Aristotle to Frank Westerman." *Nordicum-Mediterraneum* 14, no. 2. Introductory notes.

Pukan, E.S. 2016. "Haudenosee Indigenous Knowledge as Reflected in Oren Lyon's 'Where is the Eagle Seat?': An Oration to the United Nations." *Journal of Language and Literature* 16, no. 2, pp. 114–125.

Sakakibara, C. 2011. "Climate Change and Cultural Survival in the Arctic: People of the Whales and Muktuk Politics." *Weather, Climate and Society* 3, pp. 76–89.

Smith, G.N., and H.A. Wilson. Autumn 2011. "The Inuit Circumpolar Council in an Era of Global and Local Change." *International Journal*, pp. 909–921.

Smith, L.C. 2017. "Coaching for Leadership Resilience: An Integrated Approach." *International Coaching Psychology Review* 12, no. 1, pp. 6–23.

Spencer, F.W., and Y. Monterro Salvatico. n.d. *Creating Stories of Change: Reframing Causal Layered Analysis as Narrative Transformation.*

Wildman, P., and S. Inayatullah. 1996. *"Ways of Knowing, Culture, Communication and the Pedagogies of the Future." Futures* 28, no. 8, pp. 723–740.

Chapter 9

BBC. July 22, 2021. *China Floods: 12 Dead in Zhengzhou Train and Thousands Evacuated in Henan.* www.bbc.com/news/world-asia-china-57861067 (accessed July 28, 2021).

Brown, B. 2018. *Dare to Lead.* Penguin Random House, UK.

Senge, P., C.O. Scharmer, J. Jaworski, and B.S. Flowers. 2007. *Presence: Exploring Profound Change in People, Organizations and Society.* MA: Brealey Publishing.

About the Author

David Ross works as a VUCA strategist, founding boutique management consulting firm Phoenix Strategic Management (https://phoenixstrategic .com.au) during the GFC.

For close to 30 years, he has been helping leaders, organizations, and communities of all shapes and sizes thrive as they transcend the unthinkable in dealing with their most complex—and often polarizing—social, environmental, and economic opportunities, shocks, and crises. This has included guiding clients in some of the most challenging conversations experienced within society.

David has a Bachelor of Science (1st-class honors), Master's in Environmental Engineering and (Executive) Business Administration, and Graduate Certificates in Futures Thinking and Advanced Conflict Transformation. Furthermore, David is a Fellow of the Royal Society for Arts, Manufactures and Commerce, a Fellow of the Institute for Leaders and Managers, and a Certified Management Consultant through the Institute of Management Consultants.

He is currently completing the co-writing of *Beyond the Great Resignation and Great Reset: Successfully Navigating Our Societal Sea Change.* This looks at the implications of the seismic and systemic changes that are being brought to bear on our public and private organizations, their cultures, and how leaders can help their organizations to thrive in such times through genuinely valuing and developing their employees.

Index

OTHER TITLES IN THE ENVIRONMENTAL AND SOCIAL SUSTAINABILITY FOR BUSINESS ADVANTAGE COLLECTION

Robert Sroufe, Duquesne University, Editor

- *Sustainability For Retail* by Vilma Barr and Ken Nisch
- *Bringing Sustainability to the Ground Level* by Susan Gilbertz and Damon Hall
- *People, Planet, Profit* by Kit Oung
- *Handbook of Sustainable Development* by Radha R. Sharma
- *Community Engagement and Investment* by Alan S. Gutterman
- *Sustainability Standards and Instruments* by Alan S. Gutterman
- *Sustainability Reporting and Communications* by Alan S. Gutterman
- *Strategic Planning for Sustainability* by Alan S. Gutterman
- *Sustainability Leader in a Green Business Era* by Amr E. Sukkar
- *Managing Sustainability* by John Friedman
- *Human Resource Management for Organizational Sustainability* by Radha R. Sharma

Concise and Applied Business Books

The Collection listed above is one of 30 business subject collections that Business Expert Press has grown to make BEP a premiere publisher of print and digital books. Our concise and applied books are for…

- Professionals and Practitioners
- Faculty who adopt our books for courses
- Librarians who know that BEP's Digital Libraries are a unique way to offer students ebooks to download, not restricted with any digital rights management
- Executive Training Course Leaders
- Business Seminar Organizers

Business Expert Press books are for anyone who needs to dig deeper on business ideas, goals, and solutions to everyday problems. Whether one print book, one ebook, or buying a digital library of 110 ebooks, we remain the affordable and smart way to be business smart. For more information, please visit www.businessexpertpress.com, or contact sales@businessexpertpress.com.

Printed in Australia
AUHW010629171022
370267AU00004B/4

9 781637 422960